サンテックスによろしく

Say Hello to Saint-Exupéry

装　　幀 = 淺井麗子
編集協力 = iTEP Japan
前書翻訳 = James M. Vardaman
イラスト = 賀川洋 (p.10, p.28, p.40)
写　　真 = Ullstein bild／アフロ (p.13)
カバー・本文イラスト＝サン＝テグジュペリ

カバー、および本文 p.3, p.141 に利用されているサン＝テグジュペリの図版は
サン＝テグジュペリ権利継承者から原版を提供され、複製されたものです。

日英対訳で読むサン＝テグジュペリ・ストーリー

サンテックスによろしく
Say Hello to Saint-Exupéry

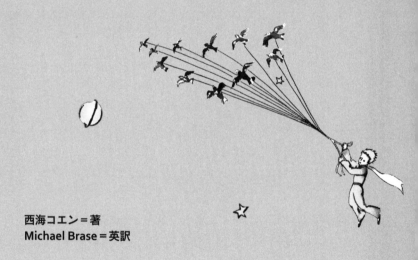

西海コエン＝著
Michael Brase＝英訳

IBCパブリッシング

まえがき

　1930年代終盤のニューヨークはすでに高層ビルが林立し、車のクラクションがそんなビルの谷間のあちこちでこだましていた。

　しかし、そんなアール・デコの装飾を競った華やいだ街角では、ヨーロッパから移住してきた人々が、せわしなく働いていた。そんな移民の一家を支えようと、半ズボンの少年が、「靴磨きをするよ」と往来で客に声をかけ、地下鉄のニューススタンドに売られている新聞は海の向こうで次第に高まる軍靴の音を伝えていた。

　海を渡ってくる人々はドイツから逃れてきたユダヤ人であり、戦火に追われたフランスや東欧の人々だった。

　彼らはそれ以前にアメリカに渡ってきて汗みずくで働く移民の先輩に混じって、祖国のアクセントが抜けきれない片言の英語で新大陸での慣れない生活をはじめていた。

　サン＝テグジュペリも例外ではない。すでに祖国フランスはヒトラーに占領され、彼の愛する飛行機は、冒険の道具から、兵士を殺傷する兵器として重宝されるようになっていた。

　皮肉なことに、戦争は文明を進歩させる。航空機も技術革新が進み、すでにサン＝テグジュペリが全身で風を感じ、全ての感覚を操縦桿の感触と頬を切る風にまかせて上下左右に翼をコントロールしていた時代が、組織に管理され、通信や機械が人を支配し始めた時代へと変化しはじめる。

　ニューヨークは、そんな時代の最先端にいながら、油まみれになって働く移民の汗の匂いと、これからの世界を動かす

Preface

In the latter part of the 1930s, New York was already filled with clusters of tall buildings and the sounds of automobile horns resounded through the canyons between them.

Within that flamboyant city, where Art Deco ornamented buildings competed for the attention of the beholders, migrants from Europe hustled about in their work. Young boys in knee breeches, trying to support their immigrant families, called out to passersby, "Shoeshine! How about a shoeshine!" while the news-stands at the subways sold newspapers that conveyed the sounds of military boots that were growing louder across the ocean.

Those who crossed the Atlantic included Jews escaping from Germany and others escaping the wartime destruction in France and eastern Europe.

This inflow mixed with earlier generations of immigrant laborers soaked in sweat who had reached America earlier. In the New World, unable to cast off the accents of their homelands, these immigrants in halting English began a new way of life to which they are unaccustomed.

Saint-Exupéry was no exception. His French homeland was already occupied by Hitler, and his beloved airplane—which he treasured as a vehicle for adventure—had become valued as a weapon, for killing and wounding enemy soldiers.

Ironically, warfare pushes civilization forward. Airplanes had undergone technological innovations. The days when Saint-Exupéry could manipulate a joystick, moving up and down, left and right, feeling with his whole being the wind that passed across his cheeks, were beginning to pass and a new age was beginning when people were managed by organizations and where communication and machinery were controlling people.

Brimming over with chaotic energy, New York was at

知性とが入り乱れた混沌のエネルギーに満ち溢れていた。それはある意味では今でも変わらない。

　サン＝テグジュペリは、フランスがドイツに占領された後、ニューヨークで『星の王子さま』をあたかも遺書のように書き上げて、そして再び彼の愛する地中海へと舞い戻った。時代に抗うように、年齢も顧みず偵察機の操縦士として飛び回り、そして最後はドイツ軍の戦闘機に撃墜され、生涯を終えたのだった。

　あちこちの星を訪ね、そこの人たちに皮肉な一言を残したり、ノスタルジックな愛情を注いだりした後で、砂漠で毒蛇に噛まれてしまう星の王子さまを描いた彼は、愛するコンスエロとの悲恋と喜劇のような毎日を思い描きながら地中海に消えてゆく。そんな彼の作品と彼の生涯とがこれほどみごとに重なり、彼の意識の中の絵物語に彩りを添えたからこそ、あの『星の王子さま』は読む人に何か不思議な思い出を植え付けてくれてきたのかもしれない。

　彼の非常識で、憎めない、今の世の中だったらどんな処遇を受けていただろうというパイロットとしての生涯が、我々の社会に問いかける何か。彼はワインを片手に現代社会で失われつつある「面白い人々」へ喝采を送っているはずだ。彼らの声に耳を傾けていると、複雑な21世紀を生きる我々もささやかな勇気をもらうのである。

　さあ、そんなことを思いながら、サン＝テグジュペリの生い立ちから最期までの素敵な物語を語っていこう。

the leading age of the times, mixing the sweaty, oil-stained immigrant laborers with the intelligence of a world to come. In a sense, that is true of the city today.

After France was occupied by Germany, Saint-Exupéry finished writing *The Little Prince* almost as a farewell note before soaring back to his beloved Mediterranean. Resisting the atmosphere of the times and paying little attention to his own age, he returned to Europe and became a reconnaissance plane pilot. His life came to an end when he was shot down by a German warplane.

After visiting a variety of planets and leaving the people he found with a number of ironic remarks and later pouring forth nostalgic affection, the Little Prince is bitten by a poisonous snake in the desert. Saint-Exupéry himself, visualizing the everyday life of tragic love and comedy with his beloved Consuelo, disappeared into the Mediterranean. His work and his life overlapped brilliantly, and that may be one reason why the illustrated book *The Little Prince* which he conceived plants such an uncanny memory in the minds of those who read it.

There is something in his life as an aviator that appeals to our world, something in his irrationality, his likeability, and his acceptance of however he is treated by the world. Surely with a glass of wine in one hand, he would offer up a toast to those "interesting people" who are gradually disappearing from present-day society. When we turn an ear to listen to him, those of us who live in this complicated twenty-first century gain a modest amount of courage.

With this in mind, let us tell the wonderful story of Saint-Exupéry from his earliest days to his demise.

アントワーヌ・ド・サン＝テグジュペリの生涯

1900年　（0歳）6月29日、5人きょうだいの長
　　　　男として、フランスのリヨンで生まれる

1904年　（4歳）父が亡くなり、母ときょうだい
　　　　で幼年時代を過ごす

1912年　（12歳）アンベリューにある飛行場で、
　　　　初めて飛行機に乗る経験をする。自作の
　　　　「空飛ぶ自転車」で空を飛ぼうとして失敗

1914年　（14歳）第一次世界大戦が勃発

1917年　（17歳）海軍兵学校を目指し受験勉強を始めるが、1919年の
　　　　兵学校の入試に失敗する。この年、郵便航空路線会社のラテ
　　　　コエールが創立される

1921年　（21歳）志願して兵役に就く。陸軍飛行連隊に所属すると同
　　　　時に、初めての単独飛行を行い、民間飛行免許を取得

1922年　（22歳）軍用機の操縦免許を取得する。秋にはルイーズ・ド・
　　　　ヴィルモランと婚約

1923年　（23歳）ル・ブールジェ飛行場を飛び立つが、墜落し重傷を
　　　　負う。タイル会社に就職。ルイーズとの婚約解消

1924年　（24歳）トラックのセールスマンとしてソーレ貨物自動車会
　　　　社に就職

1926年　（26歳）母の口利きで、アエリエンヌ・フランセーズ社の遊
　　　　覧飛行パイロットとなるが、その後、トゥールーズにあるラ
　　　　テコエール航空会社に正式に入社。姉、マドレーヌが死去。
　　　　訓練の後、トゥールーズ、バルセロナ、アリカンテ路線で郵
　　　　便物を初めて運ぶ飛行を経験

1927年　（27歳）ラテコエール航空会社が買収されアエロポスタル社

となる。カサブランカからダカールへの飛行中、飛行機の故障でサハラ砂漠に墜落（操縦は別人）。西サハラのキャップ・ジュビーの飛行場に赴任

1929年（29歳）自伝的小説『南方郵便機』を出版。その後、ブエノスアイレスに転勤し、郵便路線の開拓を担当する

1930年（30歳）同僚アンリ・ギヨメがアンデス山脈で遭難し、彼を捜索する。1週間後、ギヨメは発見される。後に妻となる、コンスエロ・スンシンに出会う

1931年（31歳）コンスエロと結婚。操縦士としての経験を書いた『夜間飛行』をガリマール書店から出版

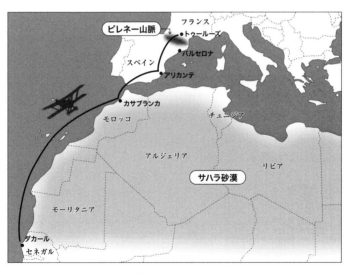

サン＝テグジュペリの南方飛行地図

若き日のサン＝テグジュペリは、南仏のトゥールーズを起点に、地中海に面したスペインの港町アリカンテ、さらに海を越えてモロッコのカサブランカ、そして西アフリカのダカールの3ヵ所を結ぶルートの郵便飛行に携わっていた。

1933年 （33歳）ラテコエール飛行機製造会社にテストパイロットとして入社。アエロポスタル社は後のエール・フランス社に吸収される。サン・ラファル湾でラテコエールのテスト飛行中、水没事故を起こす

1934年 （34歳）エール・フランスの宣伝部に入社

1935年 （35歳）レオン・ウェルトと知りあう。コンスエロと別居。パリ＝サイゴンの飛行記録に挑戦するが、サハラ砂漠に不時着騒ぎを起こし、ベドウィンの民に助けられる。3日後に生還、この時の体験が『星の王子さま』に反映されることとなる

1938年 （38歳）親善旅行中、グアテマラで離陸に失敗し重症を負う

1939年 （39歳）ガリマール書店から『人間の大地』を出版。この年、第二次世界大戦が勃発し、予備空軍大尉として招集される

1940年 （40歳）フランスがドイツに降伏すると、北アフリカ経由でアメリカに亡命。敵の攻撃を受け、ギヨメは地中海に墜落し死亡

1942年 （42歳）ニューヨークに到着後、『星の王子さま』の執筆を開始

1943年 （43歳）レオン・ウェルトに捧げた『星の王子さま』が北米で出版される。後にフランスに戻り、飛行部隊に再入隊し、フランス本土の偵察飛行を任される

1944年 （44歳）6月、偵察飛行中のエンジン故障でコルシカ島で一夜を過ごすが、そのときに多くのドイツ軍の写真を撮影。7月31日、ボルゴ基地を飛び立った後、消息を絶つ。翌月、パリが解放される

もくじ

サンテックスによろしく
Say Hello to Saint-Exupéry

『星の王子さま』を書いて空に消えた人のものがたり

The Story of the Man Who Vanished into the Sky
after Writing *The Little Prince*

1

　大きな拡声器を通して流れるハチドリの羽のような音を聞きながら、飛行機はゆっくりと滑走路を離れてゆく。プロペラの轟音と共に風が舞い、地上から浮いたと思えば、地平線のラインがゆっくりと視界にはいる。

　森はすぐには遠ざかることはなく、速度と共に風が顔面に襲いかかる。やがて、木々の枝が見えなくなると、世界はそれぞれのかたまりごとに凝縮をはじめる。

　機体が霧に覆われる。湿気が鼻腔にやわらかい香りを届け、それに気づいたとき、彼は目を前に向ける。すると雲の間から縦縞の陽光がいく筋もフロントガラスに反射をはじめた。ゆっくりと旋回。空がまわり、夕日が流れ込む。向かい風が心地よい。やがて、離陸の緊張がほぐれ、サン＝テグジュペリは少し背を伸ばして周囲を眺める。

Making a sound like the wings of a hummingbird amplified by a large loudspeaker, the plane slowly leaves the runway. Its propeller roars; the wind swirls. Slowly, as if emerging from the earth itself, the line of the horizon rises into view.

The woods do not immediately fade into the distance, and with the increase in speed the wind beats furiously against the pilot's face. Eventually, as the branches of the individual trees became indistinguishable, the world begins to condense into individual clumps.

The craft is enveloped in mist. The moisture delivers a soft aroma to the nasal passages, which causes the pilot to look forward. It is then that several shafts of light began to shine through gaps in the clouds and reflect off the front glass. The plane circles slowly. The sky turns. The evening sun comes flowing in. There is a pleasant head wind. Eventually, there is a relaxation of the tension accompanying takeoff, and de Saint-Exupéry stretches his back and looks around at his surroundings.

□ runway　滑走路
□ horizon　地平線

□ Saint-Exupéry
　サン＝テグジュペリ〈人名〉

大西洋へと機体を向けた。午後の長い光と雲が作り出す影の向こうに海原がみえてくると、彼はいきなりスケッチブックをとりだした。操縦桿(かん)のことも忘れ、その瞬間を紙に描く。そのスケッチから、いい文章をひねり出したと思ったときに、それを語って聞かせる人が側にいないことにちょっとした苛立ちを覚えてしまう。

　風の音が強すぎて、後ろに搭乗している相棒にも語れない。サン＝テグジュペリは、作品を作るとき、思いついた文章を人に読んできかせる癖があった。それは子供の頃からの習慣だったが、大人になっても同じことをするものだから、周囲は大変だったという。
　「お、これはすごい」と思うと、夜中でも友人を叩き起こして読んできかせるのだ。時には何度も同じところを読み、そこで校正をしてはまた読み直すので、それに付き合わされるのは一苦労だった。でも、空の上での朗読は不可能だった。彼は一人でエンジンの音にもまけない大声を上げて思いついた文章を反復してみる。

He turns the plane toward the Atlantic Ocean. Beyond the long shafts of light and clouds of evening, the broad expanse of the sea comes into view. It is then that Saint-Exupéry suddenly pulls out a sketchbook and begins to draw the scene before him, forgetting about the control stick. Then, just when he believes he has written a good description of the scene from the sketch, he feels a bit of frustration that there is no one nearby who he can share it with.

The wind is so strong that he can't communicate with the person sitting in the cockpit behind him. When Saint-Exupéry wrote something, he was in the habit of reading it to someone nearby. That had been his habit since childhood, something he continued doing after becoming an adult, much to the dismay of those around him.

When he had written something he really liked—"Oh, this is great!"—he would wake up his friends in the middle of the night to read it to them. Sometime he would read the same place more than once; after proofreading it, he would read it again. It was hard keeping up with him. But reciting to friends was impossible above the clouds, so he repeatedly read what he had written aloud, in a voice big enough to be heard over the engine.

□ Atlantic Ocean　大西洋　　　　　　□ recite　朗読
□ proofreading　校正

12歳のころ、サン＝テグジュペリは自転車にボロ切れの羽根をつけて坂道を疾走しながら空を飛ぼうとしたことがあった。もちろん思うようにはいかず転倒する。でも、自転車が一瞬浮力を帯び、体がふわりと浮きあがったとき、サン＝テグジュペリは大人が決して感じることのできない、風にのって空へ引き込まれてゆく夢の世界にいたのかもしれない。いや、彼にとってはそれこそが夢ではなく現実だった。セーターにまいたマフラーをなびかせて、サン＝テグジュペリは地球から旅立ったのだった。

＊＊＊

　少年時代、サン＝テグジュペリはいつも風変わりなことをやってみては怪我をして、手や足に包帯をまいていたという。彼のあだ名は太陽王。金髪の巻き毛がトレードマークだった。あの「星の王子さま」にちょっと似ている。気が散漫で落ち着きがなく、学校の成績は決してよくはなかった。

　しかし、こと飛行機や機械の組み立てとなると異様な執着をもっていた。不思議なことに、機械に興味のある子供が、同時に詩や小説にも夢中で、詩作にふけることもしばしばだった。学校の先生や友達にいわせると、いつも何かを夢想しているようで集中力がなく、何を考えているのかわからなかったという。勉強をしているかと思うと、外の景色に気をとられ、窓の向こうの森をぼんやりと眺めている。彼の目には他の人にはみえないものが映っていたのかもしれない。

When Saint-Exupéry was 12, he attached some tattered feathers to a bicycle and attempted to fly by racing down a slope. Naturally, this didn't go well and he took a tumble. But for that one moment, when the bicycle became buoyant and his body floated up in the air, he perhaps experienced a world cut off from that of adults, a dreamlike world reached by riding on a cloud. But no, it was not a dream but reality. Wearing a sweater and a muffler flowing in the wind, Saint-Exupéry was setting off on a voyage from the earth.

***

During his youth Saint-Exupéry was apparently always doing something crazy, which resulted in his arms and hands being constantly covered with bandages. His nickname was the Sun King. His curly blond hair was his trademark. There is a resemblance with the Little Prince. He was easily distracted and fidgety, and his grades in school could not be called good.

However, he had a particularly avid interest in building planes and machines. It may seem strange, but the same boy who was interested in machines was also crazy about novels and poetry, and he was often seen intensely absorbed in writing poetry. According to his teachers and friends, he always seemed to be dreaming about something and lacked concentration; it was hard to tell what he was thinking. One minute he seemed to be studying; the next he was gazing distractedly at the woods outside the window. It was almost as if he could see things that others couldn't.

□ tattered　ボロ切れの 　　　　□ fidgety　落ち着きのない
□ buoyant　浮かび上がる

この性格は大人になっても変わることはなかった。パイロットとして勤務をはじめた頃、朝の出勤時に同僚と市電で待ち合わせていたことがあった。しかし、彼はいつまで経ってもやってこない。心配になってアパートに行ってみたところ、湯船につかったまま居眠りをしていたという。読みかけの本は水浸し。きっとバスタブに体を横たえて空想にふけっているうちに眠ってしまったのだろう。

　そもそもサン＝テグジュペリは早起きが大の苦手だった。時間厳守で規則正しい生活をよしとする航空業界にとってはまったくの異端児だったのだ。それでも不思議と彼は同僚や上司に好かれていた。フランスの航空の先駆者で叩き上げの上司であったディディエ・ドーラとの面接ですら、一時間も遅刻してくるような男だったのに。

　こいつは職業パイロットには向かないかもしれないと、ドーラは思ったものの、サン＝テグジュペリの機械へののめり込み方は普通でなく、整備士としては極めて優秀だったと記録されている。そしてドーラは彼の生涯の友の一人になった。

　サン＝テグジュペリは空を愛していた。彼にとって、飛行機のメカニズムやエンジンの構造、そして航空力学は論理的な科学ではなく、夢にいざなう魔法の道具だったのかもしれない。

This aspect of his character didn't change even after he reached adulthood. When he started working as a pilot, he used to meet up with a colleague to go to work every morning on the streetcar. But one morning no matter how long the colleague waited, Saint-Exupéry didn't show up. Concerned, he went to Saint-Exupéry's apartment, only to find him napping in his bathtub. A book he had been reading was soaked in water. He had probably gotten into the tub and nodded off while daydreaming.

In any case, Saint-Exupéry was not what you would call an early riser. In the aviation industry, which revered punctuality and regularity, he might be called a maverick. Nonetheless, he was liked by his supervisors and fellow workers, despite being an hour late for his job interview with Didier Daurat, pioneer in French aviation and a self-made man.

"This fellow may never make a good commercial pilot," Daurat thought, but his enthusiasm for mechanics was remarkable. It is recorded that his skills as a mechanic were preeminent. Thereafter, Daurat and Saint-Exupéry became friends for life.

More than anything, Saint-Exupéry loved the sky. For him, the plane's mechanism, the structure of the engine, and aerodynamics were not simply logical science, but rather magic tools that drew one into a dreamlike world.

□ daydreaming　空想　　　　□ mechanic　整備士
□ maverick　異端児　　　　　□ aerodynamics　航空力学
□ Didier Daurat　ディディエ・ドー
　ラ〈人名〉

1926年、26歳のサン＝テグジュペリは、整備士を経て正式に航空郵便の会社ラテコエール社のパイロットになった。姉のマドレーヌが結核で死んでまだ数ヵ月の失意の中でのことだった。

　南仏のトゥールーズを起点に、地中海に面したスペインの港町アリカンテ。さらに海を越えてモロッコのカサブランカ。そして西アフリカのダカールの3ヵ所を結ぶルートが彼の担当だった。

　以来サン＝テグジュペリは頻繁にこのコースを飛んでいた。トゥールーズとアリカンテまではおおよそ620キロ、当時の飛行機の速度は200キロそこそこなので、離着陸の手間をいれれば4時間。風向きによっては5時間を超えるフライトだった。この飛行は、当時の航空機が可能とするぎりぎりの航続距離だったようだ。

　そもそも、どうして彼のような夢想家がパイロットになれたのだろうと誰もが思う。

　確かに彼には人を惹きつける不思議な魅力があった。何か問題をおこしても、上司と直談判をすれば、いつの間にか彼の言い分が通ってしまう。しかし、それが唯一の理由だったのだろうか。

1933年、フランス、トゥールーズにて

In 1926, at the age of 26, Saint-Exupéry officially became a pilot at the airmail company Lignes aériennes Latécoère after working there as a mechanic. This took place several month after his older sister Madeleine died of tuberculous, propelling Saint-Exupéry into despondence over her death.

Starting from Toulouse in southern France, he flew along Spain's Mediterranean coast to Alicante and then across the sea to Casablanca in Morocco, and then to Dakar in West Africa. He was placed in charge of the route that connected these three locations.

Thereafter Saint-Exupéry often flew this route. The distance between Toulouse and Alicante was about 620 km, and given that a plane's speed at the time was something like 200 km/h, the total time, including landing and takeoff, was four hours. Flight time could be over five hours depending on the direction of then wind. This was about the maximum distance a plane could manage at this time.

Why on earth, the reader may wonder, did a dreamer like Saint-Exupéry become a pilot?

To be sure, he had a certain enigmatic appeal that drew people to him. When he encountered an problem, he would talk directly to his boss, and somehow his view of the matter would be accepted. However, was this the only reason?

□ Lignes aériennes Latécoère　ラ　　□ the Mediterranean　地中海
テコエール社　　　　　　　　　　　　　□ enigmatic　不思議な、謎めいた

実は、当時パイロットは極めて危険な仕事だった。飛行機は常に事故に見舞われ、パイロットを失うので、補充も大変だったという。そんな事情も作用して、サン＝テグジュペリは定期航路の職務につく。

　中世から南仏の拠点として栄えたトゥールーズ。上空からみると赤茶色の屋根が海原のように広がっている。その街並みの真ん中をガロンヌ川が南北に流れ、川の東側、町の中心部にあるサン・セルナン大聖堂を横に見ながらサン＝テグジュペリは徐々に高度を上げる。

　郵便を運ぶ定期航空サービスのパイロットは、指定された航空路に従って、できるだけ時間通りに飛ばなければならない。通常、トゥールーズを出発するのは早朝だった。午前中にスペインのアリカンテに到着し、夕方までには北アフリカにさしかかる。その後西アフリカの中でも最もアメリカ大陸に近いセネガルの都市ダカールまで空の道は伸びていた。パイロットたちはそのルートを繰り返し往復する。

　しかし、それは現在の列車や航空機のように、機械的に全てをコントロールできるようなものではなかった。それでも、1920年代から30年代初頭にかけてのフランスは、航空業界を牽引する最新鋭の飛行機とパイロットを備えた先進国だったのだ。

＊＊＊

The fact is that being a pilot then was an extremely dangerous occupation. Planes were continually meeting with accidents, and pilots were lost and hard to replace. It was in this situation that Saint-Exupéry took over the responsibilities of a regular route.

From the Middle Ages, Toulouse flourished as a center of southern France. Seen by Saint-Exupéry from above, its reddish-brown roofs spread out like the sea. In the middle of the town, running from north to south, was the Garonne River; on its east side, in the center of town, was the Basilica of Saint-Sernin, which Saint-Exupéry could see on one side as his plane gradually rose in altitude.

A pilot carrying mail on regular routes had to adhere to designated courses and fixed schedules. Ordinarily, departure for Toulouse took place in the early morning. Spain's Alicante was reached before noon and northern Africa in the evening. After that, the pilot made his way to Dakar, the capital of Senegal and the closest location in West Africa to the American Continent. Pilots would continually fly this route over and over again.

However, different from contemporary trains and airplanes, this was not done entirely by mechanical control. As it was, from the 1920s into the 1930s, France was the leading country in aviation for the most advanced planes and pilots.

***

□ Basilica of Saint-Sernin　サン・セルナン大聖堂

トゥールーズを離陸すれば、間も無く前方に山々が迫る。フランスとスペインとの国境に横たわるピレネー山脈だ。当時はそれほど高くは飛べないので、気流の不安定な山岳地帯の飛行には注意が必要だった。特に春先は風が舞って気流が安定しない。

　この地域はヨーロッパ大陸と地中海世界との境界線。文化のみならず、その風土を生み出す気候も海と大陸とが交差する複雑なもの。

　一見青々とした空の中に、無数の風の棘があって、それが飛行機に突然襲いかかる。当時サン＝テグジュペリが操縦していた飛行機は無蓋で、気流が悪くなると遮風板の外に顔を出して周囲を見ながら操縦する。『人間の土地』という随筆の最初の部分に、彼はその模様を、「風の平手打ち」と表現している。その平手打ちの余波が耳の中でこだまする。

＊＊＊

　初飛行の前日、サン＝テグジュペリは、同僚のアンリ・ギヨメから万が一のときの不時着の場所を教えてもらう。そのうえで、ピレネー越えのための飛行方法について詳しい説明を受けたという。

After taking off from Toulouse, the mountains soon loom up ahead. Along the border of France and Spain lie the Pyrenees Mountains. Since at that time, planes could not fly very high, care had to be taken when flying in unstable mountain currents. This was particularly true in early spring when swirling winds were unpredictable.

This area forms the border between the European continent and the Mediterranean world. The culture is not only complex, but its customs are complicated, being a product of local conditions produced by the interaction of land and sea.

In what appears to be a innocent pure-blue sky, there are actually innumerable devastating thorns that will suddenly attack a plane. The plane that Saint-Exupéry flew at the time didn't have a canopy, so if the weather got rough, he would stick his head outside the windshield and steer by noting the surroundings. At the beginning of his essay titled *Wind, Sand and Stars*, he describes the experience as being like a "slap in the face." The reverberations of the sound of the slap echoed in his ears.

***

On the day before his first flight, Saint-Exupéry asked his colleague Henri Guillaumet where he should make an emergency landing if he needed to. He is also said to have received detailed instructions on how to cross the Pyrenees.

□ canopy　天蓋
□ reverberation　反響、残響
□ Henri Guillaumet　アンリ・ギヨメ〈人名〉
□ emergency[crash] landing　不時着

案の定、飛行機が山岳地帯に差し掛かると乱気流のために機体は激しく上下する。しかし、サン＝テグジュペリは、下にみえる村々や、山が近づいたときにみえてきた羊を放牧する農夫の姿に、そしてところどころに広がるオレンジの木々、雪をかぶった山々や峡谷に心を奪われていた。

　眼下にみえるおもちゃのような世界には、自然と人の日々の営みがあった。パイロットはそんな町や村がゆっくりと後方に動いてゆく様子を、革の飛行服に身を包んで、狭い操縦席から一人眺める。

　その頃のパイロットは、天候や太陽の高さ、日没と夜の闇、そして高山や平原といった、まさに自然と付き合いながら飛行機を操縦する。

ピレネー越え

As expected, just as his plane approached the mountain range, it was violently shaken up and down by an air turbulence. However, Saint-Exupéry's mind was entirely absorbed by what he saw: the mountains below and the herders tending their sheep, the orange trees spreading out here and there, the snow-capped mountains, and the steep gorges.

In the toy-like world below could be seen the realm of nature and human activity. The pilot, dressed in a leather flight suit, gazed alone at all this from his narrow cockpit, watching the villages and hamlets slowly flow past.

Pilots then had to intimately know nature to fly their planes: the weather and the heights of the sun, dusk and the darkness of the night, the mountains and the plains.

□ air turbulence　乱気流　　　　□ dusk　日没、夕暮れ
□ gorge　渓谷、山あい

目視と体感こそが飛行術の全てだったと、昔を知るパイロットは語っていた。そんな勘によるフライトこそ、彼が心から愛した飛行機の世界だった。

　「風の平手打ち」のみならず、エンジンの轟音が始終耳にまとわりつくため、パイロットは、後部座席に座る相棒の指示を聞くことができない。そこで大切なことは筆談で行われる。そんな筆談の道具がスケッチブックに変わるのだ。

＊＊＊

　あの初飛行から3年が経過した。1929年9月のその日、サン＝テグジュペリは、カサブランカからトゥールーズへ向けてピレネー越えに挑んでいた。
　その年の4月には、海軍兵学校で天体から自分の位置を測定しながら飛行する天測航法を学んでいた。それは、将来大西洋を越えて南米とヨーロッパとを結ぶ航空便に挑むための準備だった。
　海軍兵学校では、同時に水上飛行機の操縦訓練も受けていたが、整備を怠ったために着水に失敗したり、海図を紛失したりするなど、あまりにもパイロットとしての適性に欠く行為が多く、不合格になっていた。そこで、とりあえずカサブランカとトゥールーズを結ぶ路線の勤務に戻っていたのだった。

One pilot who was familiar with those days said that the art of flying consisted entirely of the ability to see and the ability to feel. It was this world of flying by intuition that Saint-Exupéry loved with all his heart.

It was not only the "slap in the face" of the wind, but the roar of the engines that continually clung to his ears, that prevented the pilot from hearing instructions given by the copilot in the rear seat. This is where communication by writing assumed an important role. This took eventually became a sketchbook.

***

Three years had passed from Saint-Exupéry's first flight. On exactly that day, in September 1929, he attempted to fly from Casablanca to Toulouse by crossing the Pyrenees.

In April of that year, he studied navigation by the stars at the Naval Academy to measure his position from celestial bodies. This was done in preparation for a future flight between South America and Europe across the Atlantic Ocean.

Also, at the Naval Academy he trained in flying a seaplane, but due to improper maintenance he failed in his attempt to land on water, lost his nautical charts, and didn't meet the standards of a pilot in many other ways. He failed the course. For the time being, he returned to flying the route between Casablanca and Toulouse.

□ Naval Academy　海軍兵学校
□ celestial body　天体

ピレネー山脈に差し掛かるといつも思い出すのが、山麓に墜落して死んだ老パイロット、ピュリのことだった。『人間の土地』に、ピュリが悪戦苦闘してピレネーの風に打ち勝ってトゥールーズに戻ったときのことが描かれている。

　当時の飛行機はエンジンの故障がつきものだった。もしピレネー山脈の真上でエンジンが止まれば、あとは滑空しながら岩山に激突しないよう飛行機をなだめ、風に乗ってなんとか着陸地点を探さなければならない。

　それだけではない。無事にピレネー山脈を越え、スペインにつき、さらに海を横断できたとしても、北アフリカでそんなことになれば、まだヨーロッパの文明を受け入れていない砂漠の民に襲われないように祈りながら、どこか安全な場所に不時着しなければならなかった。

　こうした様々な理由から、航空会社はパイロットが雲海の中を飛ぶことを禁止していたと彼は物語る。雲の中をコンパス頼りに飛べたとしても、何かがおきたら、そのすぐ下に隠れる山の尾根の牙にずたずたにされてしまいかねないからだった。

　機体に不具合がおきた瞬間に、美しい山並みや遠くに伸びる川面が凶器へと豹変するのだ。

　飛行機が落ちてゆくのではない。凶器に変貌した自然の細部が、パイロットに向かって一斉に襲いかかってくるのだった。

Whenever he approached the Pyrenees, he always remembered Puri, an old pilot who died in a crash at the foot of the mountains. In *Wind, Sand and Stars*, Saint-Exupéry describes Puri's return to Toulouse after struggling mightily with the fierce winds of the Pyrenees.

Airplanes at that time were often bedeviled by engine failure. If the engine stopped just above the Pyrenees, you had no choice but to glide down, pampering the plane so as not hit any rocks, and to ride the wind in search of a landing site.

That is not all. Even if a pilot could safely cross the Pyrenees, reach Spain, and cross the sea, somewhere in North Africa he hoped he would not be attacked by desert people who had not yet accepted European civilization. Mainly, he would have to find a safe-looking place for an emergency landing.

For all these reasons, airlines banned pilots from flying in banks of clouds. Even if they managed to do it with the use of a compass, if something unexpected should happen, the plane might be ripped apart by the fangs of the mountain ridge that hid just below the clouds.

The moment an aircraft malfunctions, the beautiful mountains and the wandering river seen in the distance are transformed into fearsome weapons.

The plane doesn't simply fall to the earth. The beautiful features of nature, transformed into weapons, attack the pilot all at once.

□ bedeviled by 〜がつきまとう、 〜に悩まされる

□ pamper なだめる、満足させる

□ bank of clouds 雲海、雲のかたまり

□ ripped apart by 〜によって引き裂かれる

その激闘に敗れ、目的地に着くことなく、機体と共にずたずたに切り裂かれたパイロットの墓標が、サン＝テグジュペリが飛んだルートに沿って点在している。

＊＊＊

　終生、空との格闘にのめり込んでいたサン＝テグジュペリが生まれたのは1900年。彼の正式な名前はアントワーヌ・マリー・ジャン＝バティスト・ロジェ・ド・サン＝テグジュペリ。中世まで遡れる伯爵家の長男だったというが、家の歴史については色々な説もあるようだ。

　トニオという愛称で呼ばれ、4歳のときに父を亡くし、母方の親戚の保護を受けながら成長した。6歳でリヨンのカトリック系の学校にはいったが、その頃に既に戯曲を作ったこともあったという。

　サン＝テグジュペリが初めて飛行機に乗ったのは、あの自転車で空を飛ぼうとした12歳の時だった。夏休みにリヨンの近くにあるアンベリューの飛行場に入り浸って、飛行機の整備士が仕事にならないほど何度も質問を浴びせかける。一度気になることがあれば、納得するまで問いかけるので、周りの人は仕事にならない。それでも、なぜかサン＝テグジュペリは整備工場の人気者だった。

　そしてついに格納庫にいたパイロットにせがみ、母親の許可を得たと嘘をついて空港の周辺を飛行してもらった。

Scattered along the route that Saint-Exupéry flew are the tombstones of pilots who lost their fierce battle with nature, never having reached their destination.

***

Born in 1900, Saint-Exupéry was to devote his whole life to fighting the sky. His legal name was "Antoine Marie Jean-Baptiste Roger, comte de Saint-Exupéry." He was said to be the oldest son of a count who traced his roots as far back as the middle ages, but there are various theories about the history of the family.

Nicknamed Tonio, at the age of 4 he lost his father and was raised under the protection of maternal relatives. By the age of 6 he had entered a Catholic school in Lyon and had written a drama.

Saint-Exupéry first "flew" a plane when he was 12, trying to fly a bike down a slope. In the summer he spent a great deal of time at Amberieux airfield near Lyon, asking the mechanics so many questions that they could hardly get any work done. Once a question rose in his mind, he kept looking for the answer until he was satisfied, disturbing the work of those around him. Even so, he was a popular figure among the mechanics in the workshop.

He finally managed to get the pilots in the hangar to let him fly around the airfield, feeding them the lie that he had gotten permission from his mother.

□ count　伯爵　　　　　　　　　　　□ hangar　格納庫
□ Amberieux　アンベリュー〈地名〉

この体験は、彼にとって忘れがたいものだった。サン＝テグジュペリの初飛行は、ライト兄弟が有人飛行に成功してほんの9年しか経っていないときのこと。しかし、その9年間に航空機にはどんどん改良が加えられていた。12歳で空を体験した彼は、パイロットになることを夢見て育った。そして21歳ではじめて単独飛行をして以来、死の瞬間まで空を飛んでいた。

＊＊＊

　無事にトゥールーズに着陸した彼は、支配人室に呼ばれる。そしてブエノスアイレスへの赴任を命じられる。1929年10月のことだった。あの世界恐慌の引き金となる、ニューヨークの証券取引所での株の大暴落の直前のことだった。

　海軍兵学校での失敗もあって、さすがに水上飛行機で大西洋を横断する職務にはつけなかったが、サン＝テグジュペリはブエノスアイレスで南米地区の支配人に就任したのだった。それは突然の辞令だった。

　6日後、彼はボルドーからブエノスアイレス行きの船で出発する。この突然の異動が、彼の作家としての名前を後世に残す『夜間飛行』を生み出すきっかけとなる。彼を待っていたのは荒漠としたパタゴニアの大地の飛行だった。

This turned out to be an unforgettable experience. Saint-Exupéry's initial flight took place a mere nine years after the Wright brothers first manned flight. In that period of time, however, tremendous improvements had been made to flying machines. Having experienced the sky at the age of 12, Saint-Exupéry grew up dreaming of becoming a pilot. From his first solo flight at the age of 21 until his moment of death he would continue to fly.

***

After his successful land in Toulouse, Saint-Exupéry was called into the manager's office. He was to be posted to Buenos Aires. This was October 1929, on the eve of the New York Stock Exchange crash that triggered the Great Depression.

Due to failures at the Naval Academy among other things, he was not given the assignment of crossing the Atlantic Ocean by seaplane, but he was, on the other hand, appointed manager of the South American region based in Buenos Aires. This was an unexpected assignment.

Six days later he left Bordeaux by boat for Buenos Aires. This sudden move led to the birth of his novel, *Night Flight*, which would preserve his name for posterity. What awaited him were flights over the barren plateau of Patagonia.

□ manned flight　有人飛行　　　　□ barren　不毛の
□ Great Depression　世界恐慌

2

サン=テグジュペリといえば、誰もが思い出すのが『星の王子さま』だろう。

彼は作家とパイロットという2つの職業に就いていた。パイロットとしてヨーロッパや南米を飛び回ること。そして作家として、記者として、時にはエッセイスト、そして『星の王子さま』に掲載されている挿絵をみてもわかるように、画家としても活動した。飛行機乗りとクリエーターという二足のわらじをはいて、決して長くない人生を駆け抜けたのだった。

でも、この2つの仕事は彼の心の中で一つに溶解している。パイロットとして生きることが、そのまま彼の作品となる。

サン=テグジュペリは友人のパイロットたちについて、普通の人がこだわることとは一見無関係にみえることを大切にしている人たちだと語っているが、そんな友人からみても彼はさらに変わっていた。

空での夢想を通して、彼の五感の隅々に流れ込む飛行機とそれを包む空気の感触。その感触から芽生えた運命への挑戦や、人生や社会への風刺が作品へと変容し、文字になって届けられる。

2

However, the literary work associated with Saint-Exupéry in the minds of most people is *The Little Prince*.

Saint-Exupéry had two occupations—writer and pilot. As a pilot he flew around Europe and South America. But he was also a writer, a journalist, a sometime essayist, and, as can be seen in the illustrations of *The Little Prince*, a painter. As a pilot and an artistic creator, he wore two hats, running through a life that was not terribly long.

But in his mind these two occupations were as one. To live as a pilot was an artistic creation.

Saint-Exupéry described his fellow pilots as people who seemed unrelated to what the average person valued, but in the eyes of his friends Saint-Exupéry himself was far from ordinary.

While daydreaming in the sky, he felt the plane permeating every corner of his five senses and the texture of the enveloping air. The challenge to fate that sprouted from that feeling, and the satire on life and society, are transformed into creative works and written as words.

□ wear two hats　二足のわらじを
　はく　　　　　　　　□ satire　風刺、皮肉

饒舌なまでの描写はどれも美しく、彼の並べる文字が読者の視覚を刺激する。それは、心の中に不思議な悲しみと詩情を呼び起こす。

　あの『星の王子さま』はサン＝テグジュペリがリビアの砂漠に墜落し、九死に一生を得たときの体験から生まれたものだという。その事件は1935年の暮れにリビアでおきている。

　それにしても、彼はよく事故に遭遇する。いかに、当時の飛行機が原始的なものだったとしても、人生の最後にドイツ軍の戦闘機に撃墜されるまで、彼は何度も墜落し、不時着をし、そして幸運にも助かっている。

＊＊＊

砂漠に不時着

Each of his almost loquacious descriptions are beautiful, and the alignment of his lettering stimulates the reader's visual senses. This evokes in the heart a mysterious sadness and poetic sentiment.

The Little Prince is said to have been born from the experience of Saint-Exupéry crashing in the Libyan Desert and narrowly escaping death. The incident occurred at the end of 1935.

All in all, it seems that Saint-Exupéry had a knack for attracting accidents. Considering how primitive airplanes were at the time, he was fortunate in surviving many forced-landings and crash-landings until he was finally shot down by a German fighter in the end.

***

□ loquacious　饒舌な　　　　　　□ narrowly escape death　九死に
　　　　　　　　　　　　　　　　　　　一生を得る

最初の事故は23歳のときだった。20歳のときに海軍兵学校への受験に失敗。失望しながら、パリの美術学校の聴講生になった。勉強には余り熱心ではなく、パリのカフェやクラブに出入りし、時には子供の頃から続けていた詩や小説を書いている。

　翌年、兵役によってストラスブールにあった航空隊に配備される。それは第一次世界大戦が終わって間もない頃、世界はまだ戦火の余韻の中で揺れていた。

　サン＝テグジュペリは、軍隊で民間飛行免許と軍用操縦免許を取得した。軍隊にいながら、ストラスブールの街でアパートを借りて過ごし、時には民間航空会社の飛行機に乗せてもらったりしていた。こうした一連の行動は、軍規違反であるにもかかわらず、なぜか懲罰を受けない。
　その後も、サン＝テグジュペリはたびたび規律を破り、それを指摘されると直談判をして自分の意向を通すというのが、彼のライフスタイルとなっていった。

His first misfortune occurred when he was 23. At 20 he had failed the entrance exam to the Naval Academy. Terribly disappointed, he became an auditor at a art school in Paris. He was not a serious student, however, and spent a good deal of time frequenting Parisian cafés and clubs. From time to time he wrote poems and novels, something he had been doing since childhood.

The next year he was drafted and assigned to the aviation corps in Strasbourg. This was not long after the end of World War I, and the world was still suffering from the war's aftereffects.

Saint-Exupéry had obtained civilian and a military pilot's licenses while in the military. During that time he rented an unauthorized apartment in the city of Strasbourg and was sometimes allowed to ride on commercial airplanes. This series of actions, despite violating military regulations, was inexplicably not punished.

Afterwards as well, Saint-Exupéry often broke the rules, and when an infraction was pointed out to him, he would talk with the aggrieved party directly and win him over; this became his lifestyle.

□ auditor　聴講生
□ aviation corps　航空隊
□ aggrieved party　被害者、不当な扱いをされた当事者

そんな彼が許可も得ないままに、娯楽のために操縦した飛行機が90メートルの上空から墜落し、同乗していた少尉と共に重傷を負ったのだ。それが最初の墜落事故だった。2ヵ月の飛行停止の処分は、未熟な飛行と軍規違反という二重の責任への対価としてはあまりにも軽かった。

　一ついえることは、サン＝テグジュペリほど飛行機に夢中になっている人物はいなかったようだ。そのことが上官や周囲の情状へと繋がったのかもしれない。彼は常に人々から仕方なく許されてしまう不思議な魅力をもっていた。

＊＊＊

　その年サン＝テグジュペリは除隊し、タイル会社に就職するもののうまくいかず、ホテルを転々としながらの困窮生活を続けていた。

　お金に困ると母親に無心する。そのことが一族の間で問題にもなるほどだった。後年ブエノスアイレスの支配人になったとき、彼を厄介者として非難していた親戚に自慢しようと、母親をわざわざ南米まで呼び寄せている。

Once, without obtaining permission, a plane he was flying for the fun of it plummeted 90 meters to the ground, fortunately without serious injury to him or the officer who riding with him. This was to be the first of numerous accidents involving a crash landing. The punishment, which consisted of two months in which he was forbidden to fly, seemed too light for the double crime of reckless flying and breaking military discipline.

One thing that can be said for certain is that there seems to have been no one else as crazy about airplanes as Saint-Exupéry. Perhaps that is what tied him so closely to his superior officers and others around him. He seems to have had the rather mysterious power of getting people to forgive him for his misdeeds.

***

In the same year Saint-Exupéry was discharged from the military and got a job at a tile company. But it didn't work out, and he continued to live in poverty while moving from hotel to hotel.

When he was short of money, he would borrow from his mother. This happened so frequently that it became a problem in the family. Later, when he became manager of the Buenos Aires office, he took the trouble of bringing his mother to South America to show his relatives that he was not the good-for-nothing they had accused him of being.

□ plummet　真っ逆さまに落ちる　　□ take the trouble of 〜 ing　わざ
□ officer　将校　　　　　　　　　　わざ〜する

とはいえ、若きサン＝テグジュペリは、そんないきあたりば
ったりの生活のため、恋人ルイーズ・ド・ヴィルモランとの
婚約をヴィルモラン家の反対で破棄されてしまう。

　これは相当の痛手だったようだ。彼はその後も恋文を送り
続けるが、一度愛想をつかした女性は二度と昔の男のところ
には戻らなかった。

＊＊＊

　サン＝テグジュペリがやっとのことで再就職したのは24歳
のときだった。就職先はパリ郊外にあるソーレというトラッ
クの販売会社。そこではトラックのエンジンの整備や分解に
夢中になったという。その後田舎に配属され、トラックの販
売員になるものの、営業実績は皆無。

　しかしそんなことはお構いなしで、田舎の風景や人々の素
朴な暮らしを堪能し、詩や小説を書いていたという。営業所
のボスは詩が好きで、彼に好感をもち、おそまつな営業態度
にもかかわらず、解雇されることはなかったというから面白
い。

　その後、サン＝テグジュペリはパリに戻るものの、パリでの
華やかな生活や社交になじめない。田舎の素朴な環境に浸っ
ていた彼には、都会での生活が虚飾にみえたのだった。

However, it was precisely the vagabond lifestyle of the young Saint-Exupéry that led to his engagement with Louise Lévêque de Vilmorin being called off, due to the objections of her family.

This was a severe blow to Saint-Exupéry. Afterwards, he continued to send her love letters, but once having fallen out of love, she wasn't inclined to fall in love with the same man again.

***

By the time Saint-Exupéry was able to find reemployment he was 24. The company was Camions Saurer, a manufacturer of trucks among other things. He became, it is said, absorbed in the maintenance and disassembly of truck engines. After that, he was assigned to the countryside and became a truck salesman, but in fact he produced no sales.

He didn't let that bother him, however. He enjoyed the scenery of the countryside and the simple life of the people; he also wrote poems and novels. It is interesting that the office manager was fond of poetry and took a liking to Saint-Exupéry, and in spite of his poor sales record, the manager never released Saint-Exupéry.

Thereafter, although he returned to Paris, Saint-Exupéry never got used to the showy lifestyle there. Having been immersed in the rustic environment of the countryside, life in the city seemed to be all show and no meaning.

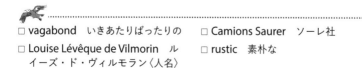

□ vagabond　いきあたりばったりの　　□ Camions Saurer　ソーレ社
□ Louise Lévêque de Vilmorin　ル　　□ rustic　素朴な
　イーズ・ド・ヴィルモラン〈人名〉

47

やはり飛行機に乗ろう。母親の知人に頼み込み、その口利きで彼はラテコエール社のパイロットになったのだった。

　12歳のときに初めて飛行機に乗り、その後、軍隊で空を飛んだ後、やっと本格的な空との出会いを果たしたことになる。1926年、26歳の秋のことだった。それは、北アフリカの砂漠との出会いでもあった。

　ルイーズとの別離の頃から若禿があり、おまけに195センチという巨体。自分の風貌にサン゠テグジュペリはコンプレックスを抱いていたという。そんな図体をもちながらも、子供の頃と同様に何を考えているかわからないようなところがあり、身勝手で遅刻や規律違反は日常茶飯事。

　考え事をするとき、部屋をのろのろと歩き回るので、まるで熊のようだったと知人は語る。しかし、一度笑みを浮かべるとその素敵な笑顔に多くの人々は怒ることも忘れてしまう。

＊＊＊

　サン゠テグジュペリはようやく天職に就くことができた。

　北アフリカの砂漠を抜け、モロッコの背骨アトラス山脈を横に見ながら西に向かえば、そこには大西洋が広がっている。そんな砂漠と大海原との接点を彼は飛ぶ。不安がなかったわけではない。

After all, flying was best. Through the good offices of a friend of his mother's, he became a pilot at Lignes aériennes Latécoère.

Having first "flown" when 12, and then taken to the skies in the army, he now encountered the heavens in earnest. This was in 1926 when he was 26 years old. It also marked his first encounter with the desert of North Africa.

About the time he separated from Louise, he began to grow prematurely bald, while physically being a formidable 195 cm tall. About his appearance, Saint-Exupéry seemed to have a complex. Though impressive in looks, it was hard to tell what he was thinking, just as when he was a child. He was self-serving and disobedient from one day to the next.

When he was mulling over some problem, he would stomp around the room much like a bear, his friends said. Yet once a smile appeared on his face, his beaming expression was so appealing that most people forgot to be angry with him.

***

Saint-Exupéry finds his calling in life.

If one flies above the North African desert and heads west looking to one side at the Atlas Mountains on the spine of Morocco, one will see the great expanse of the Atlantic Ocean. Saint-Exupéry flew along the borderline where these two expanses met. It would be false to say that he didn't feel some unease.

□ prematurely bald　若禿の　　　　　　　茶飯事
□ from one day to the next　日常　　□ calling　天職

砂漠にはヨーロッパの勢力に帰属しないムーア人が出没する。彼らは侵入者を歓迎しない。既に何人かのパイロットが犠牲になっていた。

　当時の航空機は航続距離が短かったので、北アフリカをセネガルまで飛んでゆくためには、ところどころに中継基地が必要だった。だから、そんなムーア人の出没する地域にも時には降りなければならなかった。

　1927年2月のこと、ダカールまでの飛行の途中でサン＝テグジュペリは2度目の墜落を経験する。彼は操縦こそしてはいなかったが、同僚リゲルが操る飛行機のエンジンが壊れ、砂漠に不時着したのだった。

　二人はあやうく死にかけるが、リゲルはあっさりと「これが飛行機の操縦というものさ」と言ってのけたという。

　間も無く同僚のギヨメが救援に駆けつけたものの、一人ずつしか救出できない。そこでサン＝テグジュペリが砂漠に取り残される。ギヨメは持っていた弾薬と武器、そしていくつかの缶詰を彼に残し去っていった。

***

　静かだった。遠くからガゼルが一匹、彼を見つめていた。その時サン＝テグジュペリはムーア人への恐怖を忘れていたようだ。むしろ、孤独な体験に酔いしれていた。彼の有名な言葉がそこでうまれる。私の人生は私のもので、その責任は私にあると。

The desert was infested with Moors, who did not side with the European powers and did not welcome outsiders. Already a number of pilots had met with a sad end at their hands.

At this time a plane's range was rather short, meaning that to fly over North Africa to Senegal there was need of occasional relay stations. That's why it was sometimes necessary to come to earth in areas occupied by the Moors.

In February 1927, on his way to Dakar, Saint-Exupéry experienced his second crash-landing. While he wasn't at the controls, a colleague by the name of Rigel was. Engine trouble led to a crash-landing in the desert.

The two narrowly escaped death, but Rigel dismissed the incident by saying, "This is what flying is all about."

Their colleague Henri Guillaumet soon came to their rescue, but he could only save one person at a time. Saint-Exupéry was left in the desert by himself. Guillaumet gave Saint-Exupéry all the ammunition and weapons, as well as a number of canned goods, in his possession.

***

The desert was very quiet. In the distance a gazelle eyed him steadily. Saint-Exupéry seems to have forgotten his fear of the Moors. Rather he seemed to have become intoxicated by the solitary experience. Some of his famous sayings came into being here. For example: My life is my life; I am the one responsible for it.

□ relay station　中継基地
□ intoxicated　酔いしれて

すると、ギヨメが夕方にひょっこりと戻ってくる。近くにフランス軍の駐屯所があるという。そこを守っていたのは老下士官で、15人のセネガル兵を率いていた。

　ほとんど人と会うこともない、パリどころかカサブランカの光すら遥か彼方の砂漠の駐屯所で、久しぶりにフランス人の来訪を受けた伍長は涙を流していたとサン＝テグジュペリは記している。

　その伍長とチュニスやダカールでの恋愛談を語り合い盛り上がる。果てしなく広がる砂漠はすでに闇に沈み、その上に固定された無数の星がまたたいていた。

＊＊＊

　「星の王子さま」はそんな星のどこかにいる。きっと後年作品を手がけたとき、この砂漠での体験を思い出したに違いない。彼は自分を見舞った危機をいつも五感で吸収し、静かに詩情の中で発酵させた。そして、そこに自然と人とを一つに捉えたセンテンスを生み出し、それを幾重にも文章の中に織り込みながら表現した。

　人間も自然の一部に過ぎない。空を飛ぶ時は、ちょうどサファリの中を無防備なままに歩くようなものだと彼はいう。

　ある時は自然の美しさに包み込まれ、あるときはそんな気まぐれな自然というライオンに追われるシマウマと同じような状況に陥った。

Then what should happen but Guillaumet showed up that evening. There was said to be a French garrison nearby. It was manned by an elderly French noncommissioned officer leading 15 Senegalese soldiers.

Saint-Exupéry wrote that the French corporal, who hardly ever met a fellow countryman at this desert garrison, much less in Casablanca or even more distant Paris, was so moved by his French visitors that tears came to his eyes.

He and the corporal had a great time exchanging stories about their love affairs in Tunis and Dakar. The seeming endless desert spread out into the black of the night, and high above numerous stars twinkled in their fixed positions.

***

The star in The Little Prince was one of these stars. Years later, when he came to write the work, he most certainly recalled this experience. Whenever he was visited by danger, he always greeted it with all five senses and quietly fermented it in a poetic brew. From this he would create writings in which nature and man were woven into one fabric and given expression.

Human beings are nothing more than a part of nature. In Saint-Exupéry's opinion, to fly is like going on a safari without adequate protection.

At one time he would be enveloped by the beauty of nature; at other times he would fall into a fickle situation similar to that of a zebra being chased by a lion.

□ garrison　駐屯所
□ corporal　伍長

□ fickle　気まぐれな

しかし、自然の猛威の中にあっても、パイロットはライオンを恨みはしない。ライオンを見つめながら、いかに無事な場所に身を隠し、仲間がやってくるのを待つかを考える。

　パイロットのそうした自然との見つめ合い、そして脅威からの逃走。恐怖と同居することで逆に命を意識し、それを必死でつなぐことが、彼が表現する「闘い」だった。

＊＊＊

　彼の同僚は素晴らしい飛行機乗りだった。先輩のパイロットであったギヨメは、サン＝テグジュペリが新米だったころ、これから飛ばなければならない航路について事前に講義をしてくれる。

　しかし、あまり論理的な説明はしない。スペインにはいると、草原の中にある一本の木がみえる。その脇にある農家をみつけたら、もうピレネーを越え、風も穏やかになるはずだというふうにサン＝テグジュペリに語る。

　カサブランカに朝つけば、朝から開いている小さな飲み屋がある。そこに座って闘いの疲れを癒すのだと。

　草原があるから不時着できるかといえば、そこには小川がある。

But even faced with the ravages of nature the pilot does not begrudge the lion. Watching the lion, he thinks how to find the safest possible place to hide until his friends arrive.

The pilot's hard gaze into the face of nature, his escape from its threat. By living with fear, he was ever more conscious of life and the desperate need to connect with it. This was the "fight" he referred to.

***

Saint-Exupéry's fellow pilots were wonderful flyers. When Saint-Exupéry was still wet behind the ears, Guillaumet, who was senior to him, would give him preparatory lectures on the routes he would have to fly thereafter.

However, his explanations would not be particularly theoretical. He would explain, for example, that when entering Spain, one would see a solitary tree in a grassy plain. When one found a certain farmhouse nearby the tree, one should have already crossed the Pyrenees and the wind should have become much gentler.

If one arrived at Casablanca in the morning, there was a small pub already open where one could sit and rest one's bones from the fight.

Since there was a grassland, you would think that a forced landing would be no problem. The difficulty was, there was also a small hidden river.

□ wet behind the ears　新米の、未熟な

一見オアシスにみえた草原に隠れる小川が毒ヘビのように着陸した飛行機の足元に噛み付いてくる。ギヨメはそんな風に語りながら、要所要所についての注意を喚起する。

　友の語りは、サン=テグジュペリに地理学者や航空学者が語ってくれる理屈とは比較にならないイメージを与えてくれた。出発前のギヨメの航路解説が、彼の心の中に、そして空想の中に、これから見えてくるはずの全ての光景を、絵心をもって埋め込んでゆく。

＊＊＊

　もちろんサン=テグジュペリはパイロットだ。だから科学を否定し、詩作ばかりをして飛んでいたわけではない。むしろ状況は逆だった。彼はパイロットとして生きながら、飛行機という機械を操ることが好きだった。彼は飛行機乗りとして文章を書いていたのだ。

　パイロットは向こうに雲や山がみえたとき、普通の人間がみるのとは全く異なった感覚でそれを知覚する。この感覚を最も心得ていたのも彼だったのかもしれない。

　実は、彼はパイロットになる訓練を受けていた折、理論の方が得意で、実技はそれほどどうまくはなかったといわれている。

At first the grassland might look heaven-sent, but if a plane lands there, the hidden river bites its legs like a poisonous snake. Speaking in this way, Guillaumet would call Saint-Exupéry's attention to each important point, one after another.

The way Guillaumet explained geography and aeronautics to Saint-Exupéry was incomparably more useful that the logic of experts. The commentary on the routes that Guillaumet provided before takeoff implanted in his mind and heart and in his imagination all the sights soon to be seen.

**

But, of course, Saint-Exupéry was a pilot. That's why he didn't deny science and spend all his time flying and writing poetry. If anything, the case was the opposite. While making a living as a pilot, he loved being at the controls of the machine known as a flying machine. As an airman, he was also a writer.

When a pilot sees clouds or mountains in the distance, he perceives them with an entirely different sensibility from that of the ordinary man. The person who possessed this sensibility to the greatest degree was probably Saint-Exupéry.

The fact is that when he was undergoing training to become a pilot, he is said to have excelled in theory and not been very good in practical matters.

□ heaven-sent　神の恵みの、願ってもない

ともかく注意散漫で、気移りが激しく、緻密な行動を求められるパイロットとしては、その技量に疑問が残る。

　しかし、山腹にたなびく雲、海から香ってくる潮の香りの強弱にいかに彼が敏感だったかは、彼の小説を読めばよくわかる。

　やがて夜間飛行にはいろうとするときに、いきなり剣を振り回しパイロットを生死の狭間に追い込む大自然の軍団が待ち受けていることを彼は敏感に察知する。そして風や雲の微妙な動きから、それらが攻撃をしかけてくる前に派遣された斥候かどうか、サン＝テグジュペリは常に肌で感じようとしていた。そんな危険を察知すれば、彼は方向舵を調整し、飛行ルートの変更を考える。

　ギヨメやその後大西洋の横断に成功するメルモーズといった、当時のフランスの航空業界の花形パイロットと共に、中継基地と交信し、その夜におこりうる天候の変化を予測する。しかし、そんな盟友ギヨメもメルモーズも、サン＝テグジュペリよりも早く、空で帰らぬ人となっている。ギヨメは1940年に、イタリアの戦闘機の機銃掃射を浴びて戦死。メルモーズは、大西洋を横断中に交信を絶ったまま行方不明になっている。

　世界が次の戦争へと突き進もうとした1936年の暮のことだった。ギヨメの死から4年を経て、サン＝テグジュペリも彼らのあとを追うことになる。

In any case, he was absentminded, easily distracted, and questionable whether he possessed the meticulous skills required of a pilot.

However, if you read his novels, you realized how sensitive he was to the clouds hovering on the mountainsides and to the intensity of the smells brought in by the sea.

When he eventually was ready to undertake night flying, he keenly perceived that nature was an army of sword-wielding warriors that was determined to drive him into the valley of death. From the slightest movement of wind or clouds Saint-Exupéry could always tell by feeling alone whether they were meant as scouts for an imminent attack. If he should detect such a danger, he would make adjustments with the rudder and think about changing the route.

Together with the star French pilots of the time, such as Guillaumet and Mermoz, who subsequently succeeded in crossing the Atlantic Ocean, he communicated with relay stations and predicted possible weather changes for that night. Guillaumet and Mermoz met their end in the air much before Saint-Exupéry. In 1940 Guillaumet was downed by machine-gun from an Italian fighter. Communication with Mermoz was lost as he was crossing the Atlantic.

It was nearing the end of 1936, when the world was readying itself for another world war. Four years had passed since the death of Guillaumet, and Saint-Exupéry was to follows shortly.

□ meticulous　緻密な
□ scout　斥候

□ rudder　方向舵
□ Mermoz　（ジャン・）メルモーズ
　〈人名〉

3

　一言でいえば、サン゠テグジュペリは、伯爵家の御曹司である。いいとこのお坊ちゃんといったほうがあたっているかもしれない。人は、苗字の表記から、サン゠テグジュペリの背景が何かを理解したはずだ。

　しかし、彼はそんなことにはまったく頓着しない。服装にも気を使わず、レストランに行くときに、エンジンをいじったあとの油に汚れた手を洗おうともしない。

　軍隊の将校や、高級官僚などといった貴族の子弟の進む道には興味を持たず、むしろ伯爵家の出身という理由で接してくる人を疎んでいた。

　しかし、周囲の人々は、なんで貴族の「お坊ちゃま」がパイロットになったのかと興味を持って接していたのかもしれない。だからこそ、変わり者のパイロットというイメージが、彼の風貌や仕草と絡まって、彼につきまとったのだろう。

***

3

Saint-Exupéry was the eldest son of a count. Or it might be more appropriate to say that he was the spoiled oldest son of a well-to-do family. People could generally determine his background from a list of noble families.

But that type of thing didn't concern him in the least. He wasn't concerned about his clothing, and he went to restaurants without washing his hands just after working on an oily engine.

He had no interest in following the lead of many aristocratic scions to become a military officer or government official. Rather he avoided people who approached him because he was of aristocratic descent.

However, it is undoubtedly true that some people approached him out of curiosity as to why the pampered son of a good family should become a pilot. For that very reason perhaps, the image of the pilot as an odd character followed him around, mixed with his unique physical features and gestures.

***

□ spoiled son of a well-to-do
　family　いいとこのお坊ちゃん

□ scion　名門の子孫、御曹司
□ pampered son　お坊ちゃま

砂漠への不時着と帰還のあと、サン＝テグジュペリはデング熱にかかり、妹の住む地中海に面したアゲでしばらく療養する。そんな彼のところにアエロポスタル社の経営を任されていたドーラから連絡がはいる。

　1927年にラテコエール社は、事業の大部分をアエロポスタル社に売却していた。今のエールフランスの前身だ。サン＝テグジュペリが受けた命令は、飛行ルートの中継地点である西アフリカのキャップ・ジュビーというところへの赴任命令だった。

　皮肉なことに、ドーラはサン＝テグジュペリの貴族ならではの名前に注目していた。ドーラは、アントワーヌ・マリー・ジャン＝バティスト・ロジェ・ド・サン＝テグジュペリという彼の名前についている「ド」こそは、彼が貴族の子弟である証だと知っていた。

　本人はそうしたことを一切口にしなかったが、そもそも、彼がラテコエール社のパイロットになったのも、母親のつてを通してであれば仕方がない。

＊＊＊

　西サハラにあるキャップ・ジュビーは、スペインの軍事刑務所がぽつんとあるだけの大西洋に面したさいはての地だった。アエロポスタル社は、そこを中継地として運営するために、スペイン側とうまくやってゆかなければならない。

After the crash-landing in the desert and his return home, Saint-Exupéry came down with dengue fever and stayed with his sister in Agay on the Mediterranean for a while to recover. It was there that he was contacted by Didier Daurat, who had been put in charge of the aviation company Aéropostale.

In 1927 a good part of Latécoère was sold to Aéropostale, forming the forerunner of today's Air France. Saint-Exupéry's orders consisted of his assignment to Cape Juby in North Africa, one of the airline's stopover points.

Paradoxically, Daurat paid some attention to Saint-Exupéry's aristocratic name. Daurat knew that the de in Saint-Exupéry's full name—"Antoine Marie Jean-Baptiste Roger, comte de Saint-Exupéry—was a testament to his aristocratic birth.

Saint-Exupéry himself never spoke of such matters, but the fact is that it would not be surprising if he got the job of pilot at Latécoère through his mother's connections.

***

Cape Juby, located in West Sahara, is a piece of land in the far west of Africa facing the Atlantic, whose only feature is a Spanish military penal institution. In order for Aéropostale to make use of it as a stopover point, there was need to get along well with the Spanish side.

□ Agay　アゲ〈地名〉
□ stopover point　中継地点

□ Cape Juby　キャップ・ジュビー
〈地名、現モロッコのタルファヤ〉

その施設を指揮していたスペイン人が、たまたま貴族の出身だった。そのため、そんな指揮官とのやりとりには、サン＝テグジュペリの名前と威厳が必要だとドーラは考えたようだった。

サン＝テグジュペリは再び砂漠に戻る。文字通り身一つでの旅だった。

彼は常にトランプをポケットにいれていた。飛行場でも、砂漠のテントで夜を明かす時も、気晴らしに仲間に手品を披露する。それはあの不器用な男とは思えない、なかなかものだったという。

西サハラこそは、砂漠の民ムーア人が、スペインにもフランスにも従わず、昔ながらの生活をおくっているところだった。そんなムーア人にとって、郵便を満載した飛行機は宝物だった。パイロットを人質にとれば身代金も要求できる。

実際、飛行機が襲撃され、捕虜になったパイロットが殺されるという事件もおこっていたことはすでに書いた。それだけよく飛行機が落ちていたのだ。

砂漠が大西洋にぶつかるキャップ・ジュビーは、そんな危険な所に加えて陸路での食料の補給は難しく、船によって命の糧が運ばれる見捨てられた土地だった。

モロッコ南西端の砂漠にある都市
タルファヤ（旧ジュビー岬）にある、
サン＝テグジュペリの記念碑

As it happened, the Spaniard who was in charge of the institution was of aristocratic birth. So in dealing with this person, Daurat thought that the name and dignity of Saint-Exupéry were needed.

Saint-Exupéry again returned to the desert. The trip proved to be a one-man show.

He always had a pack of cards in his pocket. Whether at an airfield or at night in a tent in the desert, he would entertain his colleagues with card tricks. It was hard to believe he was the same man, so clever was he with his hands.

The desert Moors in Western Sahara kowtowed neither to the Spanish nor to the French; they followed the lifestyle handed down from the past. For them, airplanes packed with mail were virtual treasure troves. And if they could take the pilot hostage, they could also demand a ransom.

In fact, as mentioned earlier, planes were often attacked and their pilots taken hostage or killed. This is an indication of how often aircraft were forced down.

Cape Juby, which was positioned where the desert met the Atlantic Ocean, was not only a dangerous place in itself but difficult to supply with food over land routes, and therefore forced to rely on shipping.

□ Spaniard　スペイン人

□ one-man show　ひとり舞台、身
一つでやること

飛行場の粗末なベッドに巨体をねじ込んで夜を明かす彼の様子は、貴族の暮らしとは程遠い。そこにいたのはフランス人の整備士3名とムーア人が10名少々、あとはキキという名の猿と猫、そして犬とハイエナ。

＊＊＊

　当時のアエロポスタル社の主力機は、ブレゲー14という第一次世界大戦のころに制作された複葉機だった。はじめて作られたときは、世界初の金属製の飛行機として、フランス軍の偵察や爆撃機として使用された。

　飛行機がムーア人の住んでいるところに不時着し、パイロットが人質になると彼はにわかに忙しくなる。解放してもらうために、砂漠の奥まで行き、自らも着陸地点を探してなんとか砂漠に降下する。そして、ムーア人とやりとりをして、仲間や時には外国のパイロットまでも救出する。

　彼は通訳一人をつれてひょっこり現場にやってくる。やがて、ムーア人の間でも彼は知られるようになる。時にはムーア人を飛行機に乗せ、その魔法のような力を見せつけることもあった。空に上がったムーア人は、きっとみたこともないフランスという国の威容に圧倒されたことだろう。

The sight of Saint-Exupéry spending the night at an airfield, his huge body squeezed into a narrow bed, waiting for the sun to come up, presented a considerable contrast to aristocratic living. What else could be found there were three French mechanics and something like ten Moors. Other than that, there was a monkey name Kiki, a cat, dog, and a hyena.

***

At the time Aéropostale's principal plane was the Bréguet 14, a biplane which had been produced during World War I. When initially made, it was considered the first metal plane and was used by the French military for reconnaissance and bombing.

When a plane force-landed in an area inhabited by Moors, and the pilot was taken hostage, Saint-Exupéry would suddenly become very busy. In order to get the pilot released, he would first have to go deep into the desert, find the spot where the plane had force-landed, and somehow land there himself. He would then bargain with the Moors and rescue the French pilots, and sometimes other country's pilots as well.

Along with an interpreter, Saint-Exupéry would suddenly show up at the site of the crash. Eventually he became well known among the Moors. Now and then he would give them a ride on his plane, showing off its magical powers. From up in the sky, the Moors were undoubtedly struck by the grandeur of France, which they had never seen before.

□ reconnaissance　偵察　　　　　　□ grandeur　威容、気高さ
□ bargain　交渉する、やりとりする

人質を救出するときは、不時着によって壊れた飛行機も修理する。そして、時には砂漠にジャンプ台のような臨時の滑走路を作って、無理やり飛行機を離陸させたこともあったという。

　人懐っこく、つかみどころのないサン゠テグジュペリの魅力は、ムーア人をも惹きつけた。彼は頻繁に砂漠の中の彼らのテントを訪ねていた。

　ある時は、彼の基地に出入りしていたムーア人の奴隷を、仲間とお金を払って解放してやった。トランプでの手品も、ムーア人を魅了した。

　その結果、なんと1年間の滞在中に14名ものパイロットを救出し、彼は一躍砂漠の英雄として知られるようになる。ギヨメやメルモーズもよくやってきた。

　3人が集まったときの夜、旅の疲れでうとうとする友人を叩き起こしては、初めて本格的にてがけた小説『南方郵便機』の草稿を読んできかせたという。この作品がきっかけで、サン゠テグジュペリは作家として世に知られるようになった。

　そして、キャップ・ジュビーでの功績もあって、彼はブエノスアイレスに赴任することになったのであった。

While rescuing the pilots taken hostage, Saint-Exupéry also repaired the planes damaged in the crash. Then, at other times, so it goes, he would make something like a ski jump in the desert to serve as a temporary runway in a desperate attempt to get the plane off the ground.

Good-natured but difficult to pin down, Saint-Exupéry had a certain charm that appealed to the Moors. He was often seen visiting their desert tents.

Once, he and some of his colleagues put up the money to buy the freedom of a Moor slave who frequented their base. Saint-Exupéry's card tricks also held the Moors spellbound.

As a result, during his one year there he rescued 14 pilots and became instantly known as a desert hero. Guillaumet and Mermoz often came to visit.

When the three of them got together at night and were nodding off from the tiring day, he would suddenly wake them up, it is said, to read a passage from a draft of his first novel, *Courrier sud*. Thanks to this book, Saint-Exupéry became renowned as a writer.

It was partly due to his record at Cape Juby that Saint-Exupéry was posted to Buenos Aires.

□ good-natured　人懐っこい、気立
　てのよい

□ difficult to pin down　つかみど
　ころのない

4

　ブエノスアイレスでの勤務は1年少々だった。ギヨメやメルモーズもすでに現地で彼の到着を待っていた。

　彼が預かる路線は南米の最南端のプンタ・アレーナスからパタゴニアの大地を経てブエノスアイレスに、さらにチリのサンティアゴからアンデスの切り立った山脈を越えてブエノスアイレスへ向かうものだった。この地域の天候は、あのピレネー越えどころのはなしではない。パタゴニアは風の強いところ。ひどいときは大型台風なみの風が舞う。風が舞うときは、飛行機が吹き上げられる石のつぶてに見舞われることもままあった。

　時には風が飛行機の速度と同じスピードで正面から襲いかかってくる。だから、どんなにエンジンを全開にしても飛行機は前に進まない。しばらく飛んで振り返ると、まだ飛行場の滑走路が見えているということもあった。

4

Saint-Exupéry's stay in Buenos Aires was to amount to a little more than a year. Guillaumet and Mermoz were awaiting his arrival there.

The route that he was to be in charge of ran from Punta Arenas, at the southernmost tip of South America, through the dry plateau of Patagonia, to Buenos Aires; and further on, from Chili in Santiago and to Buenos Aires again, flying over the towering Andes. The weather in this area was incomparable to that found in the Pyrenees. The wind in Patagonia was extremely strong. At its worst, the wind was as strong as a powerful typhoon. When it blew, it more often than not blew rocks and pebbles into the air to hit the plane.

Sometimes the plane would be opposed by a headwind traveling at the same speed as the plane, meaning that the plane made no progress even at full throttle. There were times when looking back after flying a bit, the runway of the airfield could still be seen below.

□ at full throttle　エンジン全開で

まだまだ飛行機の性能も、気象学も発展途上だったのである。コックピットは無蓋なので、風とエンジンの音で何も聞こえない。

　ついに1930年6月、あのギヨメがサンティアゴからアンデスを越えるときに遭難してしまう。当時アエロポスタル社が使用していたポテーズ25複葉機に乗ったまま、アンデス山中で消息を絶ったのだった。ギヨメの乗ったポテーズ25は、高度6,000メートルでいきなり強風に煽られて、3,000メートルも降下した。場所はアルゼンチン側のチリとの国境の近く。

　マイポ火山がどんどん眼下に迫るなか、ギヨメはアクロバットのような飛行で近くのディアマンテ湖畔の雪の上に不時着したのだった。

　崩壊した飛行機から金属の棒を拾い、それで雪をかき分けながら山を降りる。遭難から一週間。捜索隊がほとんど彼の生存を絶望視していた頃、今は山岳リゾートとして知られるサンカルロスまでたどり着き、駆けつけたサン＝テグジュペリと再会を果たしたのだった。

　友の生還がわかったとき、サン＝テグジュペリは歓喜した。そして劇的な再会をはたしたとき、どんな冒険家も真似のできないことをしたとギヨメは自慢したという。

The performance of airplanes and meteorology were still in a stage of development. The cockpits had no canopies, and the sound of the wind and the engine blotted out every other sound.

Finally, in June 1930, Saint-Exupéry's friend Henri Guillaumet met with disaster when crossing the Alps to Santiago. He went down in the mountains flying a Potez XXV, the biplane used by Aéropostale at the time, leaving no trace. The plane Guillaumet was flying at an altitude of 6,000 meters was suddenly struck by a strong wind and plunged down 3,000 meters. The location was near the border with Chile on the Argentine side.

As the Maipo volcano grew ever larger in his sight, Guillaumet pulled off some clever acrobatic tricks and force-landed on nearby snow-covered Lake Diamante.

Using a metal rod taken from the plane wreckage to clear a path in the snow, he began his way down the mountain. One week passed. Then, just as the rescue party had almost given up finding him alive, he showed up at what is now the mountain resort of San Carlos, where he met up with Saint-Exupéry, who had hurried to his side.

When Saint-Exupéry learned that his friend Guillaumet had been found alive, he was overjoyed. And when he had his dramatic reunion with Saint-Exupéry, Guillaumet bragged that he had accomplished something that no other adventurer could do.

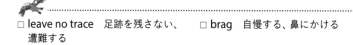

□ leave no trace　足跡を残さない、　　□ brag　自慢する、鼻にかける
遭難する

実はサン＝テグジュペリ自身もパタゴニアでは何度か命を失いかけている。そもそも強風時の着陸が大変だった。飛行機の正面を向かい風に向けると、風速と飛行機の推力とが相殺されて、空中で飛行機がほぼ止まった状態になる。そんな飛行機を竹の棒でひっかけて地上に下ろす。

　日々命がけの郵便輸送だったわけだ。しかしアエロポスタル社は、この郵便輸送事業の将来性を予測していた。もし大西洋さえ問題なく航空機で渡れ、しかも昼夜を間断なくつないで郵便物を運べれば、配達時間が以前とは比べものにならないほど短縮される。

　すでに、北アフリカとフランスとの間では夜間飛行を実施することで、速達便の配送が現実のものとなっていた。

　そして1930年5月に、大西洋に突き出したセネガルにあるサン＝ルイから、ブラジル北東部のナタールまで、ラテコエール28型水上飛行機がはじめて飛行に成功する。アフリカから南米までの横断を成し遂げたのはメルモーズだった。彼はさらにその3年後に陸上機で同じ空路の初飛行を成し遂げた。飛行機が少しずつ世界の輸送手段の先端に躍り出ようとしていたのだった。

If the truth be told, Saint-Exupéry came close to losing his life any number of times in Patagonia. First of all, it was hard to land when a strong wind was blowing. When flying directly into an headwind, the speed of the wind and the thrust of airplane cancelled each other out. The plane ended up being virtually stopped in midair. If you wanted to, you could pull it down to the ground with a hooked bamboo pole.

Every day was a day of life-risking delivery of the mail by air. Aéropostale correctly predicted the future of this business. If, however, the Atlantic presented no problems in traversing by plane, and the mail could be delivered day and night without stop, then delivery times would be immeasurably shorten.

Night flights between North Africa and France had already been put into practice, and special delivery was a reality.

Then in May 1930 the Latécoère 28 seaplane was the first to successfully fly from Saint-Louis in Senegal, which juts out into the Atlantic, to Natal in northeastern Brazil. Mermoz was the only one to successfully make a transatlantic flight from Africa to South America. He made his first flight on the same air route in a land-based plane three years later. Airplanes were bit by bit taking a leading role in the delivery of the world's mail.

□ cancel each other out　相殺する　　□ Saint-Louis　サン＝ルイ〈地名〉
□ special delivery　特別配達、速達　　□ bit by bit　少しずつ
　便

その頃、サン＝テグジュペリは、中米エルサルバドル出身の
コンスエロ・スンシンという女性と出会う。彼は、生涯にわ
たって何度か恋をしていた。特に婚約者だったルイーズの家
で知り合ったネリー・ド・ヴォギエとは、生涯友人としても
親しくしていた。そんな彼がたちまちコンスエロのエキゾチ
ックで奔放な性格に魅了される。ブエノスアイレスでは、コ
ンスエロを何度も飛行に誘っている。

　1931年2月にサン＝テグジュペリはフランスに帰国し、しば
らくして二人は結婚。しかし、彼女は贅沢好きで浪費家だっ
たようだ。サン＝テグジュペリは、彼女の作る借金のために働
いていたという人もいたほどで、そんな生活から逃避するよ
うに、彼は何度か他の女性とも恋愛を繰り返している。ネリ
ー・ド・ヴォギエは、彼にとって、そうした苦しみを癒して
くれる友でもあったのだ。

　その頃、彼は『星の王子さま』のまえがきにでてくる作家、
レオン・ウェルトとも知り合っている。

コンスエロ（1942年）

Around this time Saint-Exupéry met up with the Salvadorean Consuelo Suncín. Throughout his life he had in fallen in love a number of times. Nelly de Vogüé, in particular, whom he had met at the home of his fiancée Louise, would remain a lifelong friend. He was immediately fascinated by her exotic, bohemian ways. In Buenos Aires he took her flying a number of times.

In February 1931 Saint-Exupéry returned to France, and before long the two got married. However, Consuelo liked luxury and extravagance. Some people went so far as to say that he only worked to pay off her debts, and that he had affairs with other women to escape that type of life. Nelly de Vogüé was one of his woman friends who made life easier.

About this time he made the acquaintance of the writer Léon Werth, who appears in the preface of *The Little Prince*.

□ Salvadorean　エルサルバドルの
□ bohemian　自由奔放な
□ make the acquaintance of　～と　　知り合いになる
□ Léon Werth　レオン・ウェルト〈人名〉

同じ年に、南米での経験を題材にした『夜間飛行』は、たちまちベストセラーとなった。原稿を読んで感動した著名な作家アンドレ・ジッドが序文を書いている。しかし、この作品を読むと、一つの疑問が心に生まれる。そもそもサン＝テグジュペリは作家だったのだろうかと。

　彼は飛ばなければ書けなかった。空での、砂漠での、そして大陸でのパイロットとしての経験こそが、彼の作品の全てだった。だから、登場人物の名前は違っていても、それはフィクションとは言い難い。

　描写は美しく、言葉も洗練され、読者は常に自分がパイロットになったかのような臨場感に酔わされる。でもそれはほとんど彼が実際に体験した世界だった。だから『夜間飛行』が発表されたとき、これは小説ではないという批判にも晒される。

　サン＝テグジュペリが有名になればなるほど、彼の作品や行動を巡って、マスコミも読者も彼を好きなように持ち上げ、好きなように批判する。

　しかも、この時代は困難な時代だった。世界は大恐慌のあと、次の戦争に向けて動き出していた。ソ連も強国になり、共産主義も世界に輸出されていた。

In the same year *Night Flight*, based on his experiences in South America, became an instant bestseller. André Gide was moved when he read the manuscript and later wrote a foreword. However, one question arose in the minds of some readers when reading this book: namely, was Saint-Exupéry really a creative writer; was he a novelist?

If he hadn't flown, he couldn't have written. The book was chock-full of his experiences as a pilot: the sky, the desert, the earth. So even though the names might be different, it was hard to call it fiction.

His descriptions are beautiful, his prose refined. The reader is continually intoxicated with the feeling that he is there in that moment, that he is the pilot. But this is almost always a world that the writer himself has experienced. This is why, when first published, *Night Flight*, was criticized as not being fiction, as not being a novel.

The more famous Saint-Exupéry became, the more the mass media followed his work and behavior, either criticizing or praising it to their heart's content.

Moreover, times were hard. After the Great Depression the world was headed toward the next world war. The Soviet Union became a great power and began promoting Communism abroad.

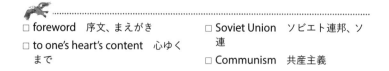

□ foreword　序文、まえがき
□ to one's heart's content　心ゆく
　まで

□ Soviet Union　ソビエト連邦、ソ
　連
□ Communism　共産主義

フランスでも、人々は右翼や左翼へと傾斜し、教養ある若者は、それぞれの思想を武器に激しい議論を繰り返していた。政界も揺れていた。そうした世情の最中に、アエロポスタル社はスキャンダルにまみれ、再編されてゆく。

　それでもサン＝テグジュペリは、パイロットとしての業務に従事するが、それはもはや昔のような孤独なものではなく、時にはジャーナリストも同行し、あのキャップ・ジュビーも取材の対象になったりした。

＊＊＊

　1930年代後半には、空の様子自体が大きく変化した。ライト兄弟がはじめて空を飛んで以来、飛行機はどんどん進化した。

　第一次世界大戦では、軍事用に改良が加えられ、その後アエロポスタル社の前身のラテコエール社などが民間輸送に航空機を利用した。

　それはフランス航空業界の黄金時代だった。しかし、やがて航空機は世界中で次世代の武器としても、輸送手段としても注目される。有名なリンドバーグの単独大西洋無着陸横断が成し遂げられたのが1927年5月。サン＝テグジュペリがキャップ・ジュビーに赴任する直前のことだった。

In France people leaned to both left and right, and the educated youth had repeated discussions using the ideas of both as weapons. The political world was in a state of turmoil. In the midst of this state of affairs, Aéropostale was caught up in a scandal and had to be reorganized.

Still, Saint-Exupéry continued his duties as a pilot, but it was not always the lonely business of the past. Sometimes he was accompanied by journalists and covered subjects like Cape Juby.

***

In the latter half of 1930, flying itself had undergone a great change. Since the Wright brothers took to the skies, flying had made tremendous strides.

In World War I, improvements were made for military use, after which the predecessor of Aéropostale, Lignes aériennes Latécoère, and others used aircraft for civilian transport.

This was the golden age of French aviation. However, it was only a matter of time before, throughout the world, airplanes came to be seen as the next generation of weaponry and transportation. It was only in May 1927 that Charles Lindbergh made his solo flight across the Atlantic. This took place immediately before Saint-Exupéry was sent to Cape Juby.

□ Charles Lindbergh　チャールズ・リンドバーグ〈人名〉

とはいえ、その頃の飛行機の操縦はまだ奔放なものだった。ちょうど大航海時代の船乗りのように、命をかけて飛行機を操りながら空を飛んでいた。

　しかし、次の世界大戦の足音が近づくにつれ、航空機にもさらなる改良が加えられ、アメリカやドイツが航空業界を凌駕するようになる。すでに20年代から、今でも営業を続けているルフトハンザのような航空会社が世界各地で設立され、成長を続けていた。

　それにつられて、パイロットの技量にもより精密な知識と規律が求められはじめていた。飛行機を操る時代から、飛行機の計器や航空規則にパイロットが従う時代へと世の中が変化していったのである。

　サン＝テグジュペリにとっては、子供の頃、自転車で空を飛ぼうとした時の、あの感触の延長に飛行機があった。そんな夢の世界が時代の進化と共に薄らいでゆく。

　そして作家としての名声が高まるなか、彼は1932年にアエロポスタル社の崩壊でパイロットを辞め、パリで執筆活動に専念するようになった。

＊＊＊

All the same, handling a plane in those days was not easy. Just as in the Age of European voyages of Discovery, pilots put their lives on the line every time they flew.

And yet as the sound of marching boots grew louder in Europe, further improvements were made in military aircraft, and the United States and Germany became the leaders in the field of aviation. By the 1920s companies like the still operative Lufthansa were established around the world and continued to expand.

Following this expansion, pilots were required to possess greater skills in terms of minute knowledge and discipline. The world had changed from an era in which planes were flown solely by the pilot's hand to an era in which pilots followed the plane's instruments and aviation regulations.

When Saint-Exupéry was a kid, an airplane was an extension of the feeling he had when he tried to "fly" on a bicycle. The world of such dreams fades with the passage of time.

With his increasing fame as a writer, he gave up piloting at Aéropostale when the company was dissolved in 1932, and took up writing full-time in Paris.

***

□ the Age of Discovery 大航海時代　　□ minute 精密な

アエロポスタル社の政治的なスキャンダルを通して、航空業会全体が再編され、エールフランスが誕生する。世界情勢が混沌としてゆくなか、サン＝テグジュペリ自身も彼の発表したエッセイや小説が彼の意図とは関係なく攻撃されたり礼賛されたりで、精神的にも穏やかではない。しかも、計画的に生活をしてゆくことに興味をもたないことから、たちまち資金難にも陥ってしまう。

　やはり空に戻りたい。彼はそう思う。

　そこで、ドーラの仲介で、飛行機製造会社として再編されていたラテコエール社にテストパイロットとして移籍した。彼は32歳になっていた。

　しかし、この仕事は一年も続かない。テストパイロットの仕事は緻密さと精密さが要求される。それは彼がもっとも苦手なことで、海軍大尉と整備士を乗せた飛行実験中に水上飛行機を墜落させたことから、彼はあっけなく解雇されてしまったのだった。

　その墜落事故では、ほとんど溺死寸前のところを救出され、臨死体験の中で死の甘美な感覚を味わったと、サン＝テグジュペリは述懐している。そんなことがあったあとでも『夜間飛行』は売れ続け、これを読んでパイロットに憧れる青年も多かったという。エールフランス社では、そんなサン＝テグジュペリに広告塔になってもらおうと考える。

***

Due to a political scandal involving Aéropostale, the entire airline industry was reorganized and Air France was born. As the world situation became more chaotic, Saint-Exupéry's newly published novels and essays were sometimes praised and sometimes criticized regardless of his intent in writing them, leaving him less than completely satisfied. Moreover, since he was not interested in living according to a plan, he soon fell into financial debt.

The sky was where he wanted to be. That is what he wanted, he thought.

So, with Daurat's mediation, he transferred to Latécoère as a test pilot, which had been reorganized as an airplane manufacturing company. He was thirty-two at the time.

However, he held this job for less than a year. What was required of a test pilot was attention to detail and accuracy—two qualities which Saint-Exupéry was particularly lacking. On a test flight with a naval lieutenant and mechanic aboard, he crash-landed a seaplane and was abruptly fired.

In this crash landing he was saved just as he was about to drown, and he later recalled the sweet sensation of this near-death experience. Even after this incident, *Night Flight* continued to sell, and after reading the book, many young people yearned to become pilots. Air France considered making Saint-Exupéry the company's poster child.

***

□ mediation　仲介　　　　　　□ abruptly　あっけなく
□ naval lieutenant　海軍大尉　　□ poster child　広告塔

サン゠テグジュペリは、ブエノスアイレスにいた頃から、時々子供のスケッチを描き始めていた。ぼさぼさの金髪をなびかせて自転車で空を飛ぼうとしていた頃。その当時の自分の姿がまぶたの内側に何度も現れた。

　そして同じ年に初めて近くの飛行場で、パイロットにせがんで飛行機に乗せてもらったときのことも思い出した。どうして？　何故？　とパイロットや整備士に質問を浴びせ続ける少年の目を描いてみる。そこには大人にはみえないものが映っていた。

　そして、あの初飛行のとき、太陽に彼の金髪が輝いていた。そんな子供の頃の自分の姿がまぶたの内側に鮮明に蘇った。彼は子供の頃に抱いていた空想の世界へ自分自身を誘ってゆく。そして、子供の頃の自分と対話をする。

　しかし、『星の王子さま』が発売されるまでは、まだしばらく時間が必要だった。今や彼はフランスだけではなく、世界中にその名を知られた作家になっていた。

　あの水上飛行機の事故以来、彼はパイロットの職を離れ、パリで作家として生活をするようになる。

From his days in Bueno Aires, Saint-Exupéry would some-times sketch the picture of a child. The drawing was of a boy with disheveled blond hair flowing in the wind. It came from the time he dreamed of flying in the air on a bicycle. An image of himself from that time often appeared in his mind's eye.

And then, in the same year at a nearby airfield, he remem-bered begging a pilot to give him a ride in a plane. He pep-pered the pilots and mechanics with endless questions: "How come? Why?" He tried to draw the eyes of the inquisitive youth. There was something there that was imperceptible to adults.

And at the time of that first flight, the sun shown down brightly on his blond hair. The image of him as a young boy was firmly imprinted on his inner eye. In effect, he was luring himself into the world of fantasy that he had known as a child. And he conversed with himself as a child.

However, before the publication of *The Little Prince*, there was still need for some time. Now his name was known as a writer not only in France, but throughout the world.

Ever since the crash of the seaplane, he had given up being a pilot and had taken up life in Paris as a writer.

□ pepper （質問などを）浴びせる
□ lure　誘い込む、誘惑する

そんなアパートにも知人がやってきて政治談義に花が咲く。共産主義に共鳴するレオンもその中にいた。しかし、サン゠テグジュペリ本人は、人に右とか左といったレッテルを貼る政治に興味を抱けない。すぐに年齢や身分、所属している組織といった外見で人を描写し、それで納得する大人の世界に、サン゠テグジュペリは少々嫌気がさしていた。

　とはいえ、生きてゆくために稼がなければならなかった。34歳になったサン゠テグジュペリは、ついにエールフランスに口説き落とされ、同社の広報を担うことになる。そもそもデスクワークをすることが嫌いな彼は、エールフランスからの誘いには難色を示していた。

　そこで、彼は特別な条件を引き出し、マスコミ向けの執筆や講演のかたわら、自らがパイロットとして役員やジャーナリストを乗せてアルジェリアに飛んだりした。

　7月にはサイゴンまでの長距離飛行を行い、現地でさらに友人とアンコールワットまで行こうとする。しかし、出発後間もなく、エンジントラブルでマングローブの中に不時着。そのときは病に侵されてしまう。

Friends came to his apartment and had political discussions. Léon Werth, who was a Communist sympathizer, was among them. Saint-Exupéry himself, however, was not interested in politics that labeled people as being left or right. He had a distinct dislike for adults who were satisfied when defining others by such external attributes as age, social status, and associated organizations.

That said, in order to keep food on the table he had to earn a living. At the age 34 he finally gave into Air France's cajoling and became head of its public relations. At first, Saint-Exupéry had not been receptive to Air France's off since he was disinclined to do deskwork.

Here Saint-Exupéry elicited some special conditions. Aside from writing and lecturing for the mass media, he would fly to Algeria and elsewhere with himself as pilot and board members and journalists as passengers.

In July he made the long flight to Saigon, and from there planned to fly to Angkor Wat with a friend. However, not long after taking off, engine trouble forced the plane down in a mangrove. This time he fell ill.

□ label　レッテルを貼る
□ cajole　口説く、丸め込む

事故の衝撃のぼんやりとした意識の中で、彼は4年前にブエ
ノスアイレスに戻る途中、フランスの国立劇場の俳優をのせ
たまま沼地に不時着したときのことを思い出す。その時は、パ
ジャマや下着、バスローブをひっかけたままの姿でブエノス
アイレスまで歩いて戻った。乱れた髪の女優の肩にオウムや
猿がのっていた。彼はマングローブの中でそんな夢想にふけ
って微笑んでいた。

　35歳のときには、新聞社の依頼でソ連を取材し、スターリ
ンが国威をかけて製造したマクシム・ゴーリキーという飛行
機にも試乗。機内には映画館や会議室まで備えられていた。彼
は素朴に搭乗を楽しんだ。ソ連の取材記事はフランスで大き
な話題となる。

　その後サン＝テグジュペリは、エールフランスと交渉し、カ
サブランカから北アフリカの諸都市を巡ってカイロまでの講
演を兼ねた遊覧飛行を企画している。
　実際は、寄港地に着けば友人と豪遊し、せっかくの講演料
を使い果たし、次の目的地に到着するときはほとんど無一文
だったという。

In his fuzzy mind after the shock of the crash, he remembered returning to Buenos Aires four years earlier carrying actors from the French National Theater and crash-landing in a swamp. At that time his only possessions were a pair of pajamas, underwear, and a bathrobe. In such attire he walked all the way back to Buenos Aires. He saw a tousle-haired actress with a monkey and parrot sitting on each shoulder. In the middle of a mangrove swamp, lost in daydreams, he smiled to himself.

At the age of 35, a newspaper asked him to visit the Soviet Union, and he even was given a test ride on the plane, called the Maxim Gorky, which Stalin had constructed with national pride. It even equipped with a movie theater and a conference room. Saint-Exupéry enjoyed the relaxed, easy flight. His coverage of the Soviet Union created quite a stir back in France.

After that, he negotiated with Air France to conduct a scenic/lecture flight from Casablanca to various cities in North Africa as far as Cairo.

In fact, once having reached his port of call, he went out on the town with his friends, spent his hard-earned lecture fee, and by the time he reached his next stop, he was completely penniless.

□ attire　装い、身なり
□ Maxim Gorky　マクシム・ゴーリキー〈人名を冠した航空機〉
□ coverage　取材、報道
□ port of call　寄港地

そうした一見華やかな生活の中でも、彼は何故か心が晴れなかった。妻のコンスエロの贅沢も続き、夫婦喧嘩も絶えなかった。

　彼は生活費がなくなると、友人にたかり、夕食を奢ってもらう。しかし、そのこと自体はそれほど辛いことではなかったようだ。そもそも、金銭に頓着することは彼にとっては潔いことではない。

　ただ、彼はそんな潔さを知人にも求めてしまう。「人は友人の役にたちたがるものだ」というフランスの哲学者モンテーニュの言葉をよく口にしていたという。

　まさに貴族のお坊ちゃんならではの、おおらかな生き様だと噂する人もいたかもしれない。

So even in the midst of a seemingly glamorous life, he was not particularly happy. His wife, Consuelo, continued her extravagant habits, and the two of them continued their quarreling.

When he ran out of pocket money, he would sponge off a friend and get treated to dinner. But this wasn't a hardship for Saint-Exupéry. Basically, he didn't consider a concern over money to be a virtue.

However, he demanded that kind of purity of mind from friends. He often repeated the words of the French philosopher Montaigne: "A friend is someone wants to be useful to others."

There may have been those who gossiped that this kind laid-back life was possible only for the spoiled son of an aristocratic family.

□ sponge off　〜にたかる
□ Montaigne　モンテーニュ〈人名〉

5

　妻との不和は、雑誌にも暴かれ、彼のソ連の報道は物議を
かもし、右翼から攻撃される。サン＝テグジュペリは、パリで
鬱々とした毎日を送っていた。

　そこで、メルモーズやギヨメは、サン＝テグジュペリを励ま
そうと、彼にフランス航空省が企画したパリとサイゴン間の
飛行記録更新に挑ませる。再びアジアへの旅がはじまろうと
していた。費用は新聞社などへの記事を掲載する約束で前借
りをする。

　サン＝テグジュペリは、出発の直前まで家を出ていったコン
スエロを探し、不眠と準備不足のまま1935年12月29日にパ
リ郊外のル・ブルジェ空港を離陸した。地中海は雨に煙って
いた。

　波立つ海面を見下ろしながら、彼と機関士のアンドレ・プ
レヴォーは北アフリカのチュニスへと向かう。あの懐かしい
北アフリカの砂漠が眼下にみえてくる。

5

His bad relations with his wife were revealed in magazines, and his coverage of the Soviet Union was controversial and led to his being attacked by right-wing political groups. Everyday life for Saint-Exupéry in Paris was a gloomy affair.

It was then that Mermoz and Guillaumet tried to encourage Saint-Exupéry to break the flight record between Paris and Saigon planned by the French Ministry of Aviation. The trips to Asia were beginning once again. The costs of the trip would be paid in advance by payment for articles in newspapers and magazines.

Until immediately before takeoff, Saint-Exupéry had been searching for Consuelo, who had left home just before his departure on December 29, 1935, from Le Bourget Airport in the outskirts of Paris. The Mediterranean was covered in a fog-like mist.

Looking down at the billowing waves, Saint-Exupéry and his mechanic André Prévost headed for Tunis in North Africa. He could see the familiar North African desert below.

□ French Ministry of Aviation　フランス航空省

□ paid in advance　前払いの

□ Le Bourget Airport　ル・ブルジェ空港

□ André Prévost　アンドレ・プレヴォー〈人名〉

チュニスを飛び立つとやがて太陽が沈み、一つ一つ星があらわれる。大地は黒々として、その闇がどんどん濃くなってゆく。

　パリでのいざこざはもう意識から消えていた。不眠での疲れも忘れ、プレヴォーがくれたコーヒーで体を温める。

　もうどこまでも、いつまでも飛んでいられそうな気分になったと『人間の土地』で、彼は語っている。

＊＊＊

　やがて東に向かう飛行機の下に、街明かりがみえてくる。サン＝テグジュペリは旋回しながら、リビアのベンガジの空港を探し、無事に着陸した。あとは漆黒の中を、無線も届かない砂漠の上空を東へ進む。

　カイロのあかりが見えるまでは、ごうごうと響くエンジンの音だけを聴きながら、月もない星空の中を他の世界と隔絶されたまま飛び続ける。

　それは彼の愛するひとときだった。

　彼の記録によれば、しばらく進むと、いきなり強い光に照らされたという。積乱雲に飛行機のあかりが反射したのだった。

　サン＝テグジュペリは、4時間半飛べばナイル川が見えてくるものと思い、高度を下げる。しかし、辺りには何もなく、厚い雲の中でさらに低く飛んでゆく。

Leaving Tunis, the sun soon sank, and the stars appeared one by one in the sky. The earth below was pitch-dark, and its ebony shade gradually grew thicker in tone.

Parisian troubles faded from Saint-Exupéry's mind. Exhaustion from last of sleep was forgotten. His body warmed up with a cup of coffee provided by Prévost.

He began to feel, he wrote in *Wind, Sand and Stars*, that he could fly as far as he wished, that he could fly as long as he wished.

***

Eventually, from under the plane as it headed east, the lights from a town came into view. Saint-Exupéry circled the site, found the airport at Benghazi in Libya, and landed safely. All there was to do after that was to proceed east through a licorice-black sky over a desert without radio contact.

Until the lights of Cairo came into view, he could only listen to the roar of the engine and continue flying through the moonless starry night, cut off from the rest of the world.

This was the moment he loved.

According to his records, he hadn't gone very far when there was suddenly a strong flash of light. The illumination from the plane had reflected off a cumulonimbus cloud.

After four and a half hours of flight, Saint-Exupéry thought he should be seeing the Nile River soon, and accordingly he lowered his altitude. However, there was nothing around to be seen, and he flew still lower through the thick clouds.

□ Benghazi　ベンガジ〈地名〉　　　　□ cumulonimbus cloud　積乱雲

あかりの反射は不気味だった。

　いやな予感がするものの、現在位置を確認するために降下を続ける。その直後に大きな衝撃に見舞われ、一瞬で全てがひっくり返った。彼の飛行機は時速270キロでリビアの砂漠に激突したのだった。

　飛行機は砂漠の尾根をずるずると蛇行し、砂の上を這いずり廻る。砂のクッションが彼らの命を助けることになる。

　彼は、深夜の砂漠で、鉄の塊になった飛行機の操縦席に座って、状況を把握しようとする。わずかなコーヒーとワイン、そしてオレンジだけが食料の全てだった。

　今、サン＝テグジュペリとプレヴォーは、どこにいるのか皆目見当もつかない砂漠の真ん中に投げ出されている。遭難機を離れることは、捜索隊の探索を考えれば危険だった。しかし、おそらく捜索隊がやって来る頃には、二人は砂漠の中でひからびているだろうと彼は思う。

　そんなとき、なぜかアンデスで遭難したときのギヨメのことを思い出す。そして、プレヴォーと共に、ただギヨメがそうしたという記憶だけで、北東へ向けて歩き出した。

パリ―サイゴン間飛行中、
サハラ砂漠に不時着（1935年）

The flashes off the clouds were uncanny.

While Saint-Exupéry had a sense of foreboding, he had no choice but to fly even lower to determine his location. In the next instant the plane received a huge shock, and everything turned topsy-turvy. His plane, traveling at 270 km/h, had crashed into the Libyan Desert.

The plane zigzagged over the ridges of the dunes, scrabbling over the sand. It was the sand that saved their lives, acting as a cushion.

In the middle of the desert, in the middle of the night, Saint-Exupéry sat in the pilot's seat of what was now a lump of iron, trying to figure out what had happened. As far as provisions were concerned, all they had was a piddling amount of coffee and wine and a few oranges.

What was clear was that Saint-Exupéry and Prévost had been hurled out into the middle of a desert, only who knows where. In the eyes of a search party it was dangerous to leave the site of an accident. Most likely, Saint-Exupéry thought that by the time the rescue party arrived, the two of them would have died in the desert from dehydration.

Every time he had such thoughts, he recalled Henri Guillaumet's survival of a crash in the Andes. Then, simply following his memory of what Guillaumet had apparently done, he and Prévost started walking toward the north-east.

□ turn topsy-turvy　ひっくり返る　　　□ piddling　取るに足りない
□ dune　砂丘、砂の小山　　　　　　　　□ dehydration　脱水

この砂漠の旅の描写は凄まじい。何度も蜃気楼に、幻影に、そして水がなければあとどれくらいで確実に死が訪れるかを意識しながら、二人はよたよたと歩き続けた。それは絶望との闘いだった。

　砂漠に足跡を残し、同じところをぐるぐると回らないための、あるいはさらに迷わないための目印にしながら、あてもなくさまよってゆく。

　死に直面しながら交わす二人の会話は滑稽ですらある。湖が蜃気楼とわかっていても、水を飲みたい一心でそこにゆくプレヴォーの姿。ついに気が狂ったかと友の言動を見つめるサン＝テグジュペリ。

　そしてわけもなく泣き出し笑い出し、パラシュートに溜まるわずかな夜露をすすろうと懸命にもがく二人。もうこれまでと思ったとき、彼らは奇跡的に砂漠の隊商に救われた。水に顔を浸したとき、神に出会ったと二人は思ったはずだ。

　面白いことに、こうした事故がそのまま記事になり、それが読者を魅了する。

The descriptions of the trek through the desert are breathtaking. Over and over they saw mirages, illusions, and counted the days before they would run out of water and most certainly be visited by death. Staggering along, they continued their fight against despair.

Wandering without aim, they left footprints in the sand so as not to walk around in circles, or as markings to keep from wandering further afield.

Confronting death face to face, the two of them had conversations that can only be described as comical. Prévost, even though he knows that the lake he sees is a mirage, is so thirsty that he is drawn toward it. Saint-Exupéry, watching his behavior, wonders if he has finally gone crazy.

The two of them sometimes burst into tears and sometimes laughter without reason, sometimes writhing frantically to sip the night dew that had accumulated in the parachute overnight. Just as they thought they had come to the end of the line, they were miraculously saved by a desert caravan. As they rinsed their faces in water, they must have felt they had encountered a divine presence.

Interestingly enough, when this incident was reproduced as-is in the form of an article, it fascinated its readers.

□ mirage　蜃気楼　　　　　　　　□ writhe　身もだえする、もがく
□ stagger　よろめく、ふらつく

だから、サイゴンまでの挑戦がたった二日で中断されても、サン＝テグジュペリは人気者だった。もちろん、彼の操縦が無謀だったという批判がなかったわけではないが、大方は彼の帰国を熱烈に歓迎した。

＊＊＊

　そして、どんな凄まじい記憶でも、時が経てばそこの風景が凝縮し、思い出の中で美しく発酵する。サン＝テグジュペリは砂漠をいつもそんな風に描写する。読者はその記事を読んで、サン＝テグジュペリを空の英雄のように讃えるのだった。『星の王子さま』の構想は、そんな記憶の中から生み出される。

　しかし、この幸運の神との出会いが一度だけではないことが凄まじい。リビアでの墜落事故の3年後、サン＝テグジュペリはアメリカ縦断を試みて、ニューヨークから飛び立ちグアテマラで遭難したことがあった。

　このときの相棒もプレヴォーだった。プレヴォーとは、彼が愛したフランスのシムーンというプロペラ機によく同乗した。ある時など、新しく開かれたサハラ砂漠の内陸を経由してダカールに至るルートの処女飛行を一緒に行なった。

　しかし、帰国するときにサン＝テグジュペリがライオンの子どもをおみやげに機内に乗せたため、プレヴォーはひっかき傷だらけでフランスに戻ってきたというエピソードも残っている。

Thus, even though the attempt to fly from Paris to Saigon had to be called off after two days, Saint-Exupéry became a popular figure. Naturally, there was some criticism of his reckless flying, but overall his return to France was enthusiastically welcomed.

***

Then there is the fact that no matter how ghastly a memory is, with the passage of time it condenses and ferments into something beautiful. Saint-Exupéry's descriptions of the desert are always beautified in this way. Reading his article of this experience, readers raised Saint-Exupéry to the status of a hero of the skies. The structure of *The Little Prince* was taken from this memory.

However, it is amazing that Saint-Exupéry's encounter with the god of good fortune should happen more than once. Three years after the crash-landing in the Libyan Desert, he attempted to fly the length of the American continent, taking off in New York and force-landing in Guatemala.

André Prévost was also Saint-Exupéry's partner on this occasion. Prévost often accompanied him in his beloved propeller-driven Simoun. At one time, the two made the maiden flight over the newly opened inland route over the Sahara to Dakar.

However, on the way back Saint-Exupéry brought back a lion's cub in the plane as a souvenir, resulting in Prévost getting terribly scratched, as one story tells it.

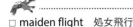

□ maiden flight　処女飛行

しかし、グアテマラでの墜落は彼の健康に決定的な打撃を与えたようだった。パンナム機によってニューヨークに戻ったサン＝テグジュペリはやつれきっていて、マンハッタンでしばらく療養し、フランスに戻ったあともしばらく休養する。

　大陸縦断のためにアメリカを訪れたとき、彼は無線飛行をはじめとしたアメリカの進んだ航空技術に感動する。

　しかし、その後再びアメリカを訪れ、ハリウッドで映画の打ち合わせをしたときなど、アメリカ社会があまりにも拝金主義に染まっているとして怒りをあらわにしたこともあった。

　ニューヨークではじめて自動ドアをみて、こんなドアがあると、今にアメリカ人は自分でドアを開けることもできなくなると毒づいた。彼はアメリカに未来をみた。でも、その未来は人の血のかよっていない殺伐としたもの。

　自分の手で操縦桿と格闘しながら空を飛び、自然と一対一で相対する時代はどんどん過去のものとなっている。サン＝テグジュペリにはそれがさびしかった。

However, the crash in Guatemala appeared to have decisive influence on Saint-Exupéry's health. He returned to New York via Pan Am, tired and emaciated. In Manhattan he recuperated for a while, and he rested for some time after returning to France.

When Saint-Exupéry went to the United States to take part in an attempt to fly the length the continent, he was surprised to see how far American technologies such as radio-controlled flight, had advanced.

However, when he visited the United States later and met with Americans in Hollywood about a movie and other things, he couldn't suppress the anger he felt at the materialism of American society.

In New York he saw an automatic door for the first time, and couldn't help but make the vitriolic comment that it wouldn't be long before Americans wouldn't be able to open doors by themselves. He had seen the future of America. But that future had no living blood; it was dreary and bleak.

The day when, flying in the sky, one would struggle with the control stick, when one was on an equal footing with nature, those days were rapidly becoming a part of the past. This made Saint-Exupéry feel sad.

□ Pan Am　パンナム (パンアメリカ　　□ vitriolic　辛辣な、痛烈な
ン航空)

彼は生活のために出版社や新聞社などに取材や記事の企画をだし、前借りをする。しかし、サン゠テグジュペリは執筆には異様な執着があって、こだわりも強く、簡単には原稿が完成しない。

　37歳のとき、パリの新聞社の要請でスペインの内戦の取材に行ったときも、なかなか記事ができあがらない。やっともってきた記事を、編集者の前で推敲しなおし、破り捨てたこともあった。
　そして、時間があれば、友人などを誘って飛行機に乗ってヨーロッパや北アフリカへと旅をした。あるときのこと、彼は終生の友人で愛人でもあるネリー・ド・ヴォギエを伴って、フライトプランも提出せずにドイツ領内を飛行した。ちなみに、グアテマラでの事故のあと、マンハッタンで療養するサン゠テグジュペリの面倒をみたのもネリーだった。
　そんなネリーとフランクフルトに向かっていると、化学工場の煙突からの異臭に驚き、近くの空港に着陸する。そこではヒトラーの親衛隊の分列行進が繰り広げられていた。

To order to make a living, Saint-Exupéry would propose projects or articles to publishers, newspapers, etc., and then get an advance on the payment due. But the problem was that he had certain extraordinary obsessions and strong fixations that prevented him from easily finishing anything to his satisfaction.

At the age of 37, when a Parisian newspaper ask him to report on the Spanish Civil War, he had trouble finishing the articles. Once, having just put the final touches on an article before the editor's very eyes, he then threw it away.

Then, when he had time, he would take friends on flights to Europe and North Africa. On one occasion, together with his lifelong friend and lover Nelly de Vogüé, he flew over German territory without a flight plan. Incidentally, after the accident in Guatemala it was Nelly who looked after him in Manhattan.

When Saint-Exupéry and Nelly were headed for Frankfurt, they were surprised by a strange smell coming from the chimney of a chemical factory, and landed at a nearby airfield. There they found Hitler's SS repeatedly marching in review.

□ Spanish Civil War　スペイン内戦　　□ SS　〈ドイツ語〉ナチス親衛隊（＝
　（1936-39）　　　　　　　　　　　　　Schutzstaffel）

突然、ドイツ人の将校がやってきてスパイ容疑がかけられる。あわやというところを、たまたまネリーにドイツ側とコネクションがあり、ドイツ人将校が飛行機に同乗するという条件で、親衛隊の挙手に見送られてフランクフルトへと移動できた。もちろんフランス大使館からは大目玉をくらうことになる。ことほどさように、サン＝テグジュペリは人騒がせなことをする。

　スペインの内戦の取材中も、戦地で不用意にタバコに火をつけて敵に気づかれたり、身柄を拘束されたときも、記者の身分証明書もパスポートもホテルに置きっ放しだったり、彼はいつもトラブルを引き起こす。サン＝テグジュペリにとってはどうでもよいことが、世間ではとても大切なことなのだ。

　だから、彼は人を政党や思想では判断しない。そのさらに向こうにある人間そのものをみようとする。『星の王子さま』にもそんな心のあり方を切々と綴っている。

Suddenly a German officer came up, and they were arrested on charges of spying. Just at this perilous moment, it turned out that Nelly had a connection with the German side, and on the condition that a German officer would ride with them on the plane, they were sent off to Frankfurt by the saluting SS. Of course, Saint-Exupéry ended up getting a good scolding from the French embassy. Thus, in this and in almost every way, he was making trouble of one kind or another.

While covering the Spanish Civil War as a journalist, he was spotted by the enemy when he lit a cigarette, and when he was taken into custody, he forgot his journalist identity card and passport at the hotel—in one way or another he was always causing trouble. What for him were matters of small importance were matters of great importance for the world.

That's why he didn't judge people by their politics or philosophy alone. He looked beyond that to the human being. In *The Little Prince* he tried sincerely to put this down on paper.

□ get a good scolding from ～か
ら大目玉をくらう

□ taken into custody 身柄を拘束
される

6

　時代は次の戦争にむかって人々の運命を押し流していた。それを誰もとめることができない。戦争は人と人とを無理やり敵と味方にわけてしまう。

　そしてお互いの中に憎悪を育む。社会そのものが戦争に向かうとき、規律が増え、人は自由を奪われ、組織に従わなければならない。

　空にも見えない管理の網が敷き詰められた。皮肉なことに、戦争は技術を進歩させる。人を殺し、人を束縛する計器や制度、そして新たな発明。それらは人間だけではなく地球そのものを覆い尽くす。

　人は数字で管理され、階級によって命の重さ軽さまでが決まってしまう。しかも、そんな戦争から逃れるためには、その戦争に勝たなければならない。

6

The times were preceding toward the next war, and the fates of people were being swept away. No one could stop it. War tears people apart, making some friends, some enemies.

Hatred grows within each individual. When society itself turns toward war, discipline becomes stronger, and freedom is lost. The organization must be followed.

In the sky too, an invisible management net is laid out. Ironically, war creates progress: new ways of killing human beings, new systems and devices for restraint, new inventions. And this applies not only to human beings but covers the earth itself.

People are managed by numbers, and their heaviness or lightness is decided by their status. Moreover, in order to escape from such wars, we must win such wars.

□ tear apart　分裂させる、引き裂く

そして、戦争に勝った新しい世界には、しっかりとそこで組み立てられた社会構造が引き継がれる。人の管理の方法、組織の動かし方。こうした社会のマネージメントと危機管理が戦争ごとに進化する。現在でもそれは変わらない。

　というよりも、現在はそんな管理社会がさらに進化して、人々はそれを今や当然のこととして受け入れ、生活している。

　ベトナムや中東、アフリカなどで戦争がおきると、人々は地球を飛び越えて宇宙から町や村を監視し、コンピューターを使って情報を分析し、その分析を相手が傍受する。それを防ごうと通信手段も進化し、ついにはネット社会へと変貌する。

　現在では、人を制御統合するためのすべての技術とノウハウが、社会全体に浸透し、民間の企業にも、日々のくらしの中にも、見えない目と防御装置がはりめぐらされている。

＊＊＊

　サン＝テグジュペリは、そんな未来をおぼろげに感じ取っていた。そのとき、彼の心にはっきりと形をもって現れた姿。それは、あの金髪の少年。12歳の時の自分だった。

　自分の分身が彼の枕元を訪れては語りかける。人間は一体何に縛られようとしているのかと。「なぜなの。どうして。わからない。教えてよ」と。

And in the new world that has won the war, the firmly constructed social structure that has resulted will be passed on. How to manage people, how to move organizations. Such social management and crisis management techniques progress with each war. It is the same today as it was in the past.

Or rather, this managerial society has advanced so far today that people now accept it as natural thing in their daily lives.

When a war breaks out in Vietnam, the Middle East, Africa, etc., people go beyond the earth and carry out surveillance of towns and villages, using computers to analyze the data, which is monitored by the other side. To prevent this, communication methods have improved and eventually been transformed into an internet society.

Nowadays, all the knowhow for controlling and consolidating people has permeated all of society, and private companies and everyday life are surrounded by unseen eyes and defensive devices.

***

Saint-Exupéry had a vague feeling that the future would be something of that nature. At the time, this vagueness took on a definite shape and form. This was the blond-headed boy. Himself around the age of 12.

His alter ego would come to his bedside and speak to him. What was it that human beings were afraid of being bound by? "Why? How come? I don't understand. Teach me."

□ surveillance　監視　　　　　　　□ permeate　浸透する、広がる
□ monitor　傍受する　　　　　　　□ alter ego　分身、もう一人の自分

サン＝テグジュペリはその少年の姿に、リビアの砂漠を、キャップ・ジュビーを、西サハラの荒野を重ねてゆく。そして、パリの、ニューヨークの、あるいはブエノスアイレスで出会った大人たちを、少年が訪ねる星に住まわせた。

　ある者は全てを命令にする王様に。ある者は全てを数字にするビジネスマンに。そして、自分は誰もこない砂漠で黙々と飛行機を修理するパイロットに。

　サン＝テグジュペリは、ドイツを訪ねたとき、人の自由を束縛するヒトラーに憤った。1939年そんなドイツがついにポーランドに侵攻し、第二次世界大戦がはじまった。やがてドイツ軍は圧倒的な武力でフランスにも迫ってきた。

　彼も戦争に勝つためには、やはり戦わなければならなかった。すでにサン＝テグジュペリは『夜間飛行』や、『南方郵便機』をはじめ、様々なエッセイや寄稿でその名は海外でも知られていた。なんと、敵国となったドイツにも愛読者がいたという。

　そんなサン＝テグジュペリが、ドイツ軍がフランスに迫るなか、召集され、後方支援に回されるものの、彼はそれが不満で、ネリーのつてを頼ってパイロットを志願する。

　しかし、それは肉体的にも無理があった。グアテマラでの事故や、それまでの度重なる過酷な飛行、そして奔放な生活は彼の体を少しずつ蝕んでゆく。

On the figure of the blond boy Saint-Exupéry would overlap and interweave scenes from the Libya Desert, Cape Juby, and the Western Saharan wastelands. The people he had met in Paris, New York, and Buenos Aires were given places to live on the stars that the little prince visited.

Some were kings who gave orders to everyone. Some were businessmen who turned everything into numbers. He himself was a pilot who quietly repaired a plane in a desert where no one came.

When Saint-Exupéry visited Germany, he was indignant at Hitler's restrictions on human freedom. Then, in 1939 Germany invaded Poland and World War II began. Before long, the German Army threatened France with overwhelming power.

Saint-Exupéry also thought that in order to win in war, one had to fight. Saint-Exupéry was already known abroad in various essays and other works, including *Night Flight* and *Courrier sud*. Most surprisingly, he was said to have fans in France's enemy country, Germany.

As Germany threatened France, Saint-Exupéry was drafted into the military and sent to provide logistic support behind the lines. He was unhappy with this, and through Nelly's connections he volunteered as a pilot.

Physically, however, it was an impossible proposition. The accident at Guatemala, the repeated life-threatening flights, and his bohemian lifestyle had gradually their effect.

□ wasteland　荒野　　　　　　　　□ volunteer　〔兵役に〕志願する
□ indignant at　～に憤りを感じる

結局、戦闘機ではなく偵察機であればなんとかやってゆけるということで、サン=テグジュペリは、パリに刻一刻と迫ってくるドイツ軍の偵察飛行を繰り返す。一度などは偵察の最中に被弾し、やっとのことでパリに戻ってきたこともあった。

　1940年6月14日に、ドイツ軍はついにパリを占領。彼はボルドーから仲間と共にアルジェリアに避難する。サン=テグジュペリは、なんとかフランスのために行動をと思うが、当時イギリスにいたシャルル・ド・ゴールとも、南フランスにあってドイツと講和したヴィシー政権ともしっくりいかない。

　その年の11月27日に親友のアンリ・ギヨメが敵機の攻撃を受けて死亡する。すでにメルモーズも大西洋で行方不明になっていた。
　あの航空郵便の英雄たちの中で彼はたった一人取り残される。サン=テグジュペリが再びアメリカへ向かったのは、その直後のことだった。
　彼はギヨメの死の前からアメリカ行きを決意し、その準備のために一度はパリに戻っている。それが彼にとって最後にみたパリとなる。

In the end, Saint-Exupéry was satisfied with a reconnaissance plane rather than a fighter, and he repeatedly flew reconnaissance missions over the German army as it approached Paris minute by minute. On at least one occasion, his plane was hit while on an observation mission, and he just managed to return to Paris.

On June 14, 1940, the German army finally occupied Paris. Saint-Exupéry and his fellow countrymen left France from Bordeaux for Algeria. Saint-Exupéry wanted dearly to do something for France, but he didn't get along with Charles de Gaulle, who was in England at the time, or with the Vichy administration, which was located in South France and had signed a peace treaty with Germany.

On November 27 of the same year, the plane of Saint-Exupéry's good friend, Henri Guillaumet, was lost when it was attacked by enemy aircraft. Mermoz had already been lost when his plane went missing over the Atlantic.

Among the early heroes of airmail delivery service, Saint-Exupéry was the only one who was now left. Not long after, he once again left for the United States.

Even before Guillaumet's death he had decided to go to the United States, and he had returned once to Paris to make preparations. That would be the last time for him to see Paris.

□ Charles de Gaulle　シャルル・ド・
　ゴール〈人名〉
□ Vichy administration　ヴィシー

政権
□ sign a peace treaty　平和条約を
　結ぶ、講和する

ヴィシー政権から許可証をもらってはいたものの、パリは
ドイツ軍の占領下にあり、街には昔の活気はない。それでも
友人を訪ねてはカフェに行き、別れを惜しんだ。

＊＊＊

　その頃、彼は頻繁にアメリカを訪れている。あのグアテマ
ラでの事故で遭難したのが1938年。そして、その翌年もギヨ
メの勧めで、飛行艇でニューヨークを訪れ、一度フランスに
帰国したあと、再び船でアメリカに向かっている。
　アメリカに向かう船上にギヨメの飛行機が現れ、空から船
長に「サンテックスによろしく」とメッセージを送った。サン
テックスとは彼の終生のニックネームだ。

　アメリカでは、リンドバーグ夫妻とも交流していたが、そ
のときに第二次世界大戦がはじまり、サン＝テグジュペリは急
遽帰国したのであった。
　ギヨメが死んだとき、自分が生き残っているのは、単なる
確率の問題で、たまたま自分は不時着でき、弾も避けられた
にすぎないと彼は思う。

In spite of having received a permit to travel from the Vichy government, Paris was, after all, occupied by the German army and possessed none of its old liveliness. Still, Saint-Exupéry visited his friends and went to cafés with them, saying his last goodbyes.

***

In those days he often visited America. The wreck in Guatemala took place in 1938. The next year, on Guillaumet's recommendation, he visited New York in a flying boat, and after once returning to France, he took a boat to the United States.

As the boat was making its way through the water, Guillaumet's plane appeared above with a message for the captain: "Give my best to Saint-Ex." Saint-Ex was Saint-Exupéry's lifelong nickname.

While in the United States he was on close terms with Charles and Anne Lindbergh, but this was interrupted by the commencement of World War II, which caused Saint-Exupéry to immediately return to France.

When Guillaumet died, Saint-Exupéry thought that the fact that he was still alive was just a matter of probability: he had managed by chance to make a crash landing, and he had managed to dodge some bullets.

□ Charles and Anne Lindbergh
リンドバーグ夫妻（チャールズと
アン）

□ dodge 避ける、素早くよける

そして戦火に追われるように、サン＝テグジュペリは再びアメリカに向かっている。大西洋の波をみながら、彼はいいようのない孤独に苛まれた。時代は確実に彼をおきざりにしていった。

＊＊＊

　すでに1939年に出版された『人間の土地』はアメリカでは『風と砂と星と』という題名で発売され、ベストセラーになっていた。そんなこともあり、ニューヨークは彼を温かく迎え入れた。

　祖国を追われ、亡命したフランス人たち。アメリカにはそんな人々がド・ゴール将軍の支持者と、独裁色が強いド・ゴールに反対する人々などに分かれて、対立し、お互いにサン＝テグジュペリに支持をもとめた。

　ドイツという共通の敵に向けて、彼がどんなメッセージをだそうとしているのか注目される。彼はドイツと闘いたかった。しかし、政治の中にはいって、その色で自分が塗られるのは嫌だった。

　偵察飛行をしていたときに、パリの陥落を決定的なものとした、フランス北部のアラスの戦いを眼下にみたサン＝テグジュペリ。無数の高射砲の槍が突き上げられてくる中で、彼は全ての筋肉と神経を集中し、戦友を励ましながら右へ左へと偵察機をあやつりながら飛行を続けた。

Now, as if pursued by the fires of war, Saint-Exupéry was once again headed for America. Gazing at the waves of the Atlantic, he felt an inexpressible loneliness. Most definitely, he was being left behind by the times.

***

His previously published *Terre des hommes* (1939) came out under the English title *Wind, Sand and Stars*, to become a bestseller. Taking this into consideration, it is no surprise that the US should give him a warm welcome.

French exiles and French defectors—in the United States there were many such people, divided between supporters of General de Gaulle and those opposed him and his strong autocratic tendencies and who broke off in opposition, or who sought Saint-Exupéry's backing.

For their mutual enemy what message did Saint-Exupéry have? That was their principal interest. Saint-Exupéry wanted to fight Germany, but he didn't want to enter politics and be besmirched in a particular political color.

While on a reconnaissance flight, he saw below him the decisive moment when Paris fell at the Battle of Arras in northern France. As countless anti-aircraft guns were thrust up like spears toward him, Saint-Exupéry concentrated every muscle and nerve and continued to fly, manipulating his reconnaissance aircraft to the right and left and encouraging his comrades.

□ besmirch　汚す　　　　　　　□ comrade　仲間、同志

121

『戦う操縦士』という小説の中で、彼は「1秒ごとに生命が研ぎ澄まされる。私は生きている。生命に満ちている」とはるか下にいる敵をみながらそう思ったと記している。彼はあのアンデスやピレネーでの体験を、再び身体中に蘇らせていたのだった。政治に加わるより、その方がサン＝テグジュペリには合っていた。

　彼は政治論議に明け暮れるアメリカに住むフランス人を次第に敬遠し孤立してゆく。しかし、そんな彼が、タクシーに乗るときも、レストランで注文するときもフランス語しか話さない。

　きょとんとするウエイトレスの姿を楽しんでいるのか、フランス語がまだ十分に勉強できていないからという屁理屈をあえていうためなのか、真意はわからない。しかし、彼はフランス語に固執した。やはりフランスの気高き貴族の末裔なのだろう。

　彼は、フランスに残してきた人々のことを考える。ガブリエル・サン＝テグジュペリという妹。あのフランスの地中海岸の町アゲに住んでいる妹だ。彼女は兄の最大の理解者だった。ニューヨークで彼はそんな妹のことを考えた。そして、ユダヤ人だったレオンのことも気になった。レオンの妻はパリでドイツ軍への抵抗を密かに続けていた。

　妻のコンスエロとはとうに別居状態。そんな彼にも愛人はいた。シルビアという人妻と中華街でよく食事をした。そして、やがてあのネリー・ド・ヴォギエもニューヨークにやってきた。

In the novel *Flight to Arras* he writes, "Every single second my life is sharpened to a finer point. I am alive. I am full of life." Looking down on the enemy far below, these thoughts went through his mind, he wrote. He was reliving the experiences he had lived though in the Andes and Pyrenees. This, rather than politics, suited his temperament.

As time went on, he gradually avoided and isolated himself from the French living in the US who spent most of their time discussing politics. On the other hand, when riding in an taxi or eating at a restaurant, he spoke only French.

Whether he did this to enjoy the blank look on the waiter's face or whether it was simply a means of saying that the French language should be studied more diligently, it is hard to say. But it is true that he adhered to French. Perhaps it was because he was after all the descendant of a French aristocrat.

Saint-Exupéry often thought of the people he had left back in France. One was his younger sister, Gabrielle, who lived in Agay on the French Riviera. She was his greatest fan and supporter. In New York he often thought of her. He also worried about Leon Werth, who was a Jew. Werth's wife remained in Paris, working underground against the German army.

Saint-Exupéry and his wife, Consuelo, had long been living separately. He had a lover named Silvia. He was often seen with her, having dinner in China Town. Eventually Nelly de Vogüé also came to New York.

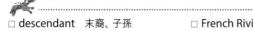

□ descendant　末裔、子孫

□ French Riviera　コート・ダジュール（＝Cote d'Azur）〈地名〉

そんなときに、コンスエロがひょっこりアメリカにやってくる。彼女はニューヨークでも派手な男女関係の噂が絶えず、奔放で贅沢な生活を続けていた。そして、サン＝テグジュペリはサン＝テグジュペリで勝手に気の合う女性とニューヨークを楽しんでいたようだ。

＊＊＊

　『戦う操縦士』がアメリカで絶賛される。ドイツ占領下のフランスでは、この作品がユダヤ人の友を描いているために発禁処分になるなど、作品の波紋が広がる。

　サン＝テグジュペリは『星の王子さま』の挿絵を何枚も描きだした。うまく描けないと、それは紙飛行機の航空編隊となって、ニューヨークのアパートの窓から飛び出した。

　1942年にはカナダにも旅をしている。出入国への準備などせずに出国したものだから、その後しばらくカナダ側に留め置かれることになるが、そんなとき、モントリオールのホテルでついに『星の王子さま』の執筆をはじめることになる。

カナダ、モントリオール近郊にて
ボートの旅の途中（1942年）

To this menagerie was added Consuelo, who suddenly showed up in America. Rumors of her extravagant relations with men were endless, and she continued her bohemian, unrestrained life as before. As for Saint-Exupéry, he did as he pleased, enjoying New York with the women he enjoyed.

***

When his novel *Flight to Arras* was published, it was highly lauded. In occupied France at the time, the book was taken to be a description of a Jewish friend and therefore banned, causing even greater waves of notoriety.

For *The Little Prince* Saint-Exupéry drew a number of illustrations. But they weren't good enough, and he flew them in formation as paper planes out of the window of his New York apartment.

1942 found him traveling in Canada. He had made the proper preparations for leaving the country but not for entering Canada. The result was that he was detained for some time by the authorities. It was then, in a hotel in Montreal, that he began writing *The Little Prince*.

□ fly in formation　編隊飛行する　　　□ Montreal　モントリオール〈地名〉

喧嘩を繰り返しながらも、なぜか決別することのないサン＝テグジュペリとコンスエロ。二人はニューヨークの東に長く伸びた島、ロングアイランドに家を借りて、夫婦喧嘩をしながらも同居する。そこで、サン＝テグジュペリは風船を飛ばしたり、浴槽の水でスープまがいのものを作ったり、子供のような仕草を楽しんでいた。

　遠い昔の金髪の少年が、精霊となって彼の心の中に宿ったのかもしれない。彼のところを訪れる友人は、派手な夫婦喧嘩とサン＝テグジュペリの不思議な行動、そしていつもの通りの、ほとんど客を無視した原稿の草稿の読み聞かせに当惑する。それでもアメリカの友人は、そんなサン＝テグジュペリが次に生み出す作品を楽しみにしていた。

　すでにアメリカも日本と開戦したことで、世界大戦の一翼に組み込まれていた。しかし、アメリカ在住のフランス人と距離をおいていたサン＝テグジュペリ。彼は結果として、愛国心のないやつだと非難される。

　そんな面倒はうんざりであったはずだ。それでも、著名人だったサン＝テグジュペリは、フランスの団結を訴え、アメリカの軍部には北アフリカからフランスを奪還する作戦を提案する。はては、おもちゃを作っていたときに思いついた新型潜水艦のアイデアまでを軍部に披露したという。

While Saint-Exupéry and Consuelo continued to have fights, for some reason they never broke up. The two of them had rented a house on Long Island, a lengthy stretch of land east of New York, and were living there together, fighting all the while. Saint-Exupéry would fly balloons in the air, make a pseudo soup with bath water, and do other kinds of childlike games.

It may be that the blond boy from the distant past had turned into a spirit and had come to resided in his heart. Friends who came visiting were confounded by the couple's extravagant quarrels and Saint-Exupéry's strange behavior, as well as by his customary reading of the manuscript draft that virtually ignored his guests. Still, one American friend said that he looked forward to Saint-Exupéry's next reading.

By that time America had already declared war against Japan and was playing an important role in the worldwide conflict. However, Saint-Exupéry kept his distance from the French people living in the United States. People criticized Saint-Exupéry, an expatriate Frenchmen, as being unpatriotic.

He must have grown tired of such talk. But as a celebrity he called for French unity and proposed a strategy for the American army to retake France from North Africa. In the end, he introduced the military to a new idea for submarines that he had come up with when making paper toys.

□ pseudo　まがいものの、偽物の　　□ submarine　潜水艦
□ unpatriotic　愛国心のない

軍事専門家や政治家は、そんな空想家のいうことは取り上げない。さらに彼はラジオなどで、政治を乗り越えたフランスの結束を訴え、アメリカ政府にもフランス救援のための手紙を書いたりするが、ド・ゴール派と反ド・ゴール派との対立の間にあって、彼の提案に賛同する者はほとんどいなかった。

　ドイツに対する連合軍の反撃がはじまろうとしていた頃、ついにサン＝テグジュペリも北アフリカへ旅立とうと決心する。1943年に『星の王子さま』が刊行。序文にユダヤ人として潜伏しているレオン・ウェルトへの思いを綴って、彼にこの本を献呈すると書き記す。

　『星の王子さま』は発行されて間もなくアメリカで大反響となっていた。そんな声援に背を向けるように、彼はアメリカを去り、アルジェリアに向かったのだ。これがコンスエロとも、ネリーとも最後の別れとなる。旅立つ決心をしたサン＝テグジュペリを、コンスエロが泣き喚いて引き止めたというエピソードが残っていた。

Military experts and politicians had no use for such pie-in-the-sky ideas and turned him down. Furthermore, on the radio and by other means, he pleaded for a French unity that went beyond politics; he also wrote to the American government asking for aid on the behalf of France. But since he was caught between the pro-de Gaulle and anti-de Gaulle factions, he found few who agreed.

Just about the time the Allied forces were preparing to counterattack the Germans, Saint-Exupéry had finally made up his mind to leave for North Africa. Around this time, in 1943, *The Little Prince* was published. In the preface Saint-Exupéry dedicates the book to the Jewish author and friend Léon Werth, then in hiding.

The book became an immediate bestseller upon publication in the United States. However, as if to turn his back on this renown, Saint-Exupéry left America for Algeria. This would be his final goodbye to both Consuelo and Nelly. It is said that Consuelo wailed and moaned in her attempt to stop him from going.

□ pie-in-the-sky idea 非現実的な
考え

□ Allied forces 連合軍

7

　アルジェでは、昔、北フランスで一緒に戦った仲間と劇的な再会となり、おおいに盛り上がる。しかし、フランスはすでにドイツの管理下におかれている。そのためサン＝テグジュペリの所属するフランス人部隊はアメリカ軍と合流し、その指揮下にはいることになった。当然のことだろうが、アメリカとしては、サン＝テグジュペリを広告塔として使いたかった。危険の多い空へ飛んでゆくより、政府の広報として彼の知名度と文筆力を活用したかったのだ。誰もがその方が彼も喜ぶと思っただろう。しかし、サン＝テグジュペリは飛行機にこだわった。

　彼の年齢で、しかも体調もすぐれない彼を、高度1万メートルを飛ぶ偵察機に搭乗させることは、軍規の上からも難しかった。

7

In Alger he had a dramatic reunion with fellow aviators who fought with him in northern France. By then France was under German administration. As a result, the French troops to which Saint-Exupéry belonged joined the US military and came under its command. It was perhaps only natural that the American army wanted to use Saint-Exupéry as a poster child. Rather than have him fly about in risk-filled skies, they wanted to exploit his fame and literary talents. Everyone thought that would please him best. However, Saint-Exupéry wasn't ready to give up flying so easily.

At his age, and given his less-than-excellent physical condition, it would be difficult to have him fly reconnaissance flights at altitudes of 10,000 meters, even taking military regulations into account.

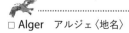
□ Alger　アルジェ〈地名〉

実際、ニューヨークにいた頃から、体に痛みがあり、時には高熱もでる。腎臓も相当悪かったようだ。しかし、サン＝テグジュペリはいつもの執拗な交渉でなんとか飛行の許可をとる。

　操縦に失敗し、やはり地上にいるようにと命令されたときなど、連合軍を指揮するアイゼンハワー将軍にも連絡をとり、あまりにしつこく迫るため、ともかくうるさいので、好きにさせてやれと側近にこぼしたと将軍の伝記に記されている。

　サン＝テグジュペリは終生サン＝テグジュペリだった。

　彼の飛行服の装着は大変な作業だった。巨体をなかなか包み込むことができず、常に周囲に手伝ってもらってなんとか飛行の準備を整える。

　しかも、新鋭の飛行機はコックピットもコンパクトなので、サン＝テグジュペリの体はなかなかおさまらない。整備士などが集まって皆で飛行機に押し込んでの離陸だった。

In fact, since his time in New York, he had suffered from various physical ailments and a high temperature. And his kidney seems to have been in fairly bad condition. But through persistent negotiation he managed somehow to get permission to fly.

After making mistakes in navigation and being ordered, in the end, to stay on the ground, he called the commander of the Allied Forces, General Dwight Eisenhower, and pressed his case. According to the General's biography, he told one of his aides that Saint-Exupéry was so obstinate and such a nuisance that they would be better off letting him do what he wanted.

From beginning to end, Saint-Exupéry was Saint-Exupéry.

Putting on his flight suit was a huge job. He couldn't easily get his enormous body into the suit to get prepared for the flight without the help of those around him.

Moreover, the cockpits of the latest planes were very compact, and Saint-Exupéry's body refused to fit in. Takeoffs were only possible when mechanics and others got together and pushed him in.

サン=テグジュペリは、空港で離陸前に司令官や管制官から受けた細かい規則を空耳で聞いてはいたが、空にあがり、太陽と風が彼を包み込んだ瞬間に、既に詳細は覚えていない。そして、もう地上との交信は聞いてはいなかった。そもそも彼は英語がよく聞き取れない。しかもヘッドフォンが嫌いだった。ヘッドフォンをつけていても頭が痛いだけだと彼はぼやく。

　彼は常に自分で飛行機を操りたかった。飛行機に操られたくはなかった。上空でヘッドフォンをむしり取ったとき、誤って窓から落としてしまったこともあった。

　そんな彼であったが、なぜかいつものように周囲の人気者だったことには変わりない。そして、さらに不思議なことに時々華々しい手柄もたてている。あまりふらふらと飛行していたために、ドイツ軍がまさかこれが敵機とは思わなかったのではといわれているが、着陸して偵察機が写したフィルムをみると、そこにドイツ軍の基地の詳細が見事に写っていたという。

　しかも、そのことを本人はまったく記憶していない。彼は地上ではなく、雲や空、そして遠い地平線を眺めていたのだった。

***

Before taking off, Saint-Exupéry would half-heartedly listen to the detailed instructions given by the commander and control officer at the airstrip, but once up in the air, the moment the sun and wind enveloped him, he forgot all the detailed instructions. Furthermore, he did not maintain communications with earth; in any case his understanding of spoken English was poor. Also, he disliked the use of headphones. He grumbled that they only gave him a headache.

Saint-Exupéry constantly said that he wanted to control the plane, not be controlled by it. Once, in flight, he ripped the headphones off his head and mistakenly threw them out the window.

Despite all this, he was still popular among those around him. More surprisingly, he would sometimes pull off a brilliant feat. For example, his plane would be wavering in flight so much that the Germans could hardly believe that it was an enemy plane, or so the story goes. However, once the reconnaissance aircraft had landed and its film checked, detailed depictions of German bases were discovered.

And yet, Saint-Exupéry had no recollection of the incident. His eyes were focused not on the earth but on the clouds and sky, on the far horizon.

***

□ half-heartedly listen　ぼんやり
　聞く
□ grumble　ぼやく、不満をもらす

□ pull off　〔困難な状況で〕うまく
　やり通す

1944年7月30日。サン＝テグジュペリはコルシカ島にいた。夜に街にくりだして、カフェで若い女性たちにトランプの手品を披露する。そして、翌朝彼は空港にやってきた。彼は空を飛びたかった。朝は相変わらず苦手で、あくびをしながら飛行場に現れた。サン＝テグジュペリはP-38に乗り込んで離陸する。離陸しながら、複葉機で南米を飛行していた頃を懐かしむ。飛行機が自分の体の一部だった頃のことをいつも思い出す。

　そして、ピカピカに磨かれた流線型の機体よりも、あのワイヤーで固定された蛾の羽根のような主翼の前についたエンジンから流れでるガソリンの匂いを嗅ぎながら、飛行機をあやつりたかった。そんな彼も今は軍人として、整備された最新鋭の偵察機を操縦する。アゲの上空を飛びたくなった。妹の住むあの家で何度不時着の後の体を休めたことか。

　実際、アメリカから帰って軍務についたあとも、彼はときどき飛行機の向きをかえてアゲの上空を飛んでいる。しかし、その日はリヨン方面へ飛ばなければならなかった。

　王子さまの星にあった美しい花を思い出す。うるさく自己主張をするものの、遠くに来てしまえばなぜか愛おしく、早く帰って水をやらなければと思う花。そして、旅立つ時に、風にあたらないように覆いをしておきたかった花。

July 30, 1944. Saint-Exupéry was on Corsica Island. At night he would spend his time in town at cafés, entertaining young women with his card tricks. The next morning he would show up at the airport. He wanted to fly. As always he was not a morning person, and he would be yawning when he made his appearance. He boarded a P-38 and took off. He fondly recalled the days in South America when he flew a biplane. He always remember the days when the plane was a part of his body.

And rather than a plane with a brightly polished stream-lined body he preferred to fly a plane in which he could smell the gas from an engine in front of moth-eaten wings that were held in place by wires. Now, as a military aviator, he wanted to fly the latest reconnaissance aircraft in the best possible condition. He wanted to fly over Agay. How many times had he stayed at his sister's house to recuperate after a crash landing?

In fact, after returning from the United States and taking up military duties, he occasionally changed the direction of his flight and flew over Agay. Of course, on those days he had to fly in the direction of Lyon.

This brings to mind the beautiful flowers depicted in *The Little Prince*—flowers that are a nuisance and annoying but endearing when seen from a distance; flowers that give rise to the feeling that one must hurry home to water them. And when one goes on a trip, flowers that one wants to cover and protect from the wind.

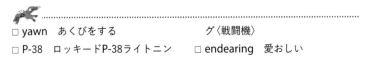

□ yawn　あくびをする　　　　　　　　　グ〈戦闘機〉
□ P-38　ロッキードP-38ライトニン　□ endearing　愛おしい

サン＝テグジュペリは、空の上でふと思う。あれはきっとコンスエロだったのだと。彼は悲しくなる。あの王子さまのように、また自分の星に戻らないと。

　砂漠を共にした友達とはすでに何度も別れてきた。メルモーズ、ギヨメ、「おい、サンテックス」と、にこにこしながら彼を呼び、何度も乾杯をし、時には朝旅立ったまま帰らぬ人となった多くのパイロットたち。そして、北フランスで機銃掃射に遭遇した戦友たち。

　郵便を積んで、カサブランカを飛び立ったときにみた夕空。そして西アフリカの砂漠やピレネー山脈の麓ののどかな町や村。そんな様々な星を彼は旅してきた。パイロットは旅人ではあるものの、名所旧跡は訪れない。ただ、時刻にしたがって、空を飛ぶ。

　どこまでも旅路は続き、やがて夜になれば無数の星と暗黒の海の間をエンジンの音だけを聞きながら飛び続ける。

　サン＝テグジュペリは、またあの星に咲く花を思った。そして次の瞬間、彼は意識を失った。後ろから迫ってきたドイツ軍の戦闘機にマルセイユ沖で撃墜された瞬間だった。それは、連合軍がフランスのノルマンディーに上陸し、ドイツ軍への攻勢をはじめた翌月のことだった。

Above the clouds Saint-Exupéry suddenly thinks to himself. That flower must be Consuelo, for sure. And he grows sad. Like the little prince, he too must return to his star.

He had already parted with any number of his desert friends—Mermoz, Guillaumet, and other pilots had called him "Saint-Ex" with smiles on their faces. They had drank to one another's health many times. There were so many pilots who left for a morning flight never to return. Not to mention his brothers in arms who fell to machine-gun fire in northern France.

Taking on a load of mail, seeing the setting sun as he left Casablanca. Then below him the West African desert and the lazy towns and villages at the foot of the Pyrenees. He has traveled through many and various stars. And while it is true that pilots are travelers, they do not visit historical sites. They just fly according to the time.

Their journey will go on forever, and eventually when night comes, it will continue between the countless stars and the darkness of the sea, the only sound being that of the plane's engine.

Again Saint-Exupéry thought of the flower that bloomed on that star. Then, in the next instant, he lost consciousness. This was the moment he was shot down by a German plane coming up from behind off Marseille. It happened the month after the Allies went on the offensive, landing at Normandy in France.

 ....

□ lazy　のんびりとした
□ Marseille　マルセイユ〈地名〉

時が経って、サン＝テグジュペリの飛行機を撃墜したドイツ空軍の兵士はいう。もし、あの飛行機に乗っていたのがサン＝テグジュペリだったら、攻撃はしなかったと。その兵士もまた、サン＝テグジュペリの空の物語の愛読者だったのだ。

1944年7月31日朝、フランスのリビエラに連合軍が上陸する二週間前、アントワーヌ・ド・サン＝テグジュペリはコルシカとローヌ峡谷の間の空中で、偵察任務の最中に消息を絶つ。彼は長きにわたってパイロットであったが、同時にライターで、そして素晴らしい哲学者でもあった。

（ニューヨークタイムズの死亡記事より）

With the passage of time, the German pilot who shot down Saint-Exupéry said that if he had known it was Saint-Exupéry in the plane, he would never have shot it down. It turned out that the German pilot was a fan of Saint-Exupéry's aviation adventures.

> *On the morning of July 31, 1944, two weeks before the Allied landings on the French Riviera, Antoine de Saint-Exupéry vanished on a reconnaissance mission in the skies somewhere between Corsica and the Rhone Valley. He had been a pilot for a long time; he was a writer, and a good deal of a philosopher.*
>
> *From obituary in The New York Times*

サン＝テグジュペリの代表作

『南方郵便機』
[仏] *Courrier Sud*

1929年に刊行されたサン＝テグジュペリのデビュー作。スペイン、モロッコ、モーリタニアを経て、ダカールにいたり、そこから郵便物が大陸へと送られていくという南米への壮大な郵便物の旅を物語る。ベルニスとジュヌヴィエーヴの愛の物語でもある。

『夜間飛行』
[仏] *Vol de nuit*
[英] *Night Flight*

1931年フランス、ガリマール書店から刊行。翌年、*Night Flight* として英訳版が刊行される。ブエノスアイレスに拠点を置くアエロポスタル社にパイロットとして勤務した経験から書かれた小説。登場人物は当時一緒に働いていた時に知り合った人々からインスピレーションを得たと言われ、特にリヴィエールは、ディディエ・ドーラがモデルとされる。1933年には映画化されたことで、さらに注目を集めることとなる。

『人間の土地』
[仏] *Terre des homes*
[英] *Wind, Sand and Stars*

1939年に出版されたエッセイ集で、サン＝テグジュペリの飛行経験が詰まっている。ラテコエール社での同僚アンリ・ギヨメに捧げた書であることでも知られている。とくにサハラ砂漠や南米のアンデス山脈を横断する危険なルートを飛行した時のエピソードは読むものを惹きつける。仲間意識や友情など、『星の王子さま』のストーリーに見て取れるテーマも含まれている。

『戦う操縦士』
[仏] *Pilote de guerre*
[英] *Flight to Arras*

ニューヨークに亡命中に書かれた小説。北フランス上空出撃の実際の体験を描いた作品で、1942年、『アラスへの飛行 *Flight to Arras*』というタイトルで英語版でも出版された。フランスが勇敢に戦ったこと、特に空軍の活躍をアメリカ人に理解させた。

『星の王子さま』
[仏] *Le Petit Prince*
[英] *The Little Prince*

1943年にフランス版と英語版、同時に出版された。童話の体裁を取りながら、詩的で、かつ哲学的な作品として、聖書についで世界で2番目に多く翻訳された作品とされている。「大人」の不条理な行動に戸惑う小さな王子との出会いが描かれている。シンプルな語りに、著者自身が描いた水彩画のイラストが深みを与えている。

参考資料

『星の王子さま』 サン＝テグジュペリ（IBCパブリッシング）

『人間の土地』 サン＝テグジュペリ 堀口大學訳（新潮文庫）

『戦う操縦士』 サン＝テグジュペリ 鈴木雅生訳（光文社文庫）

『夜間飛行』 サン＝テグジュペリ 二木麻里訳（光文社文庫）

『南方郵便機』 サン＝テグジュペリ 山崎庸一郎訳（みすず書房）

『サン＝テグジュペリの生涯』 ステイシー・シフ著 檜垣嗣子訳（新潮社）

『サン＝テグジュペリ伝説の愛』 アラン・ヴィルコンドレ著 鳥取絹子訳（岩波書店）

English Conversational Ability Test
国際英語会話能力検定

● E-CATとは…
英語が話せるようになるための
テストです。インターネット
ベースで、30分であなたの発
話力をチェックします。

www.ecatexam.com

● iTEP®とは…
世界各国の企業、政府機関、アメリカの大学
300校以上が、英語能力判定テストとして採用。
オンラインによる90分のテストで文法、リー
ディング、リスニング、ライティング、スピー
キングの5技能をスコア化。iTEP®は、留学、就
職、海外赴任などに必要な、世界に通用する英
語力を総合的に評価する画期的なテストです。

www.itepexamjapan.com

日英対訳で読むサン=テグジュペリ・ストーリー
サンテックスによろしく

2021年9月5日　第1刷発行

著　者　　西海コエン

発行者　　浦　　晋亮

発行所　　**IBCパブリッシング株式会社**
　　　　　〒162-0804 東京都新宿区中里町29番3号 菱秀神楽坂ビル9F
　　　　　Tel. 03-3513-4511　Fax. 03-3513-4512
　　　　　www.ibcpub.co.jp

印刷所　　株式会社シナノパブリッシングプレス

ISBN978-4-7946-0679-2